Tearing Down Walls
and *Building* Bridges

O. S. HAWKINS

THOMAS NELSON PUBLISHERS
Nashville • Atlanta • London • Vancouver

Published in Nashville, Tennessee, by Thomas Nelson, Inc., Publishers, and distributed in Canada by Word Communications, Ltd., Richmond, British Columbia, and in the United Kingdom by Word (UK), Ltd., Milton Keynes, England.

Unless otherwise noted, Scripture quotations are from the NEW KING JAMES VERSION or the Bible. Copyright © 1979, 1980, 1982, Thomas Nelson, Inc., Publishers.

Scripture quotations noted NIV are taken from the HOLY BIBLE, NEW INTERNATIONAL VERSION®. Copyright © 1973, 1978, 1984 by International Bible Society. Used by permission of Zondervan Bible Publishing House. All rights reserved.

The "NIV" and "New International Version" trademarks are registered in the United States Patent and Trademark Office by International Bible Society. Use of either trademark requires the permission of International Bible Society.

Library of Congress Cataloging-in-Publication Data
Hawkins, O. S.
    Tearing down walls and building bridges / O.S. Hawkins.
        p.   cm.
    Includes bibliographical references.
    ISBN 0-7852-7968-7
    1. Bible. N.T. Philemon—Criticism, interpretation, etc. 2. Interpersonal relations—Biblical teaching. 3. Christian life—Baptist authors. I. Title.
BS2765.2.H38   1995
227'.8606—dc20
                                                                        94-39493
                                                                            CIP

Printed in the United States of America

1 2 3 4 5 6 7 - 01 00 99 98 97 96 95

To Don Cavness

. . . my father-in-law and best friend, who is now in heaven. He instilled such character, confidence, and commitment in his daughter and gave me a beautiful gift on July 24, 1970, when he put her hand in mine. He knew more about "tearing down walls and building up bridges" than any man I've ever known. Paul sums up my feelings toward him when he says to Philemon:

Your love has given me great hope and encouragement because you, brother, have refreshed the hearts of the saints.

Thanks, Don. I'll see you in the morning.

TABLE OF CONTENTS

*S*ELF-HELP BOOKS ARE A DIME A DOZEN in our generation. We have a compelling need to stay ahead of the competition and to fix what is wrong in our relationships. And scores of writers have formulas and slogans to motivate and sometimes manipulate people into changing. There are volumes instructing us how to dress and how to win others to our point of view. Others offer suggestions on how to intimidate our way into relationships that can benefit us.

When it comes to the bottom line, many of today's methods of building productive relationships are superficial and deceptive—resulting in short-term gain at best.

The more advanced we become in our techniques for relating to others, the more we discover that the best ideas and methods have been proven for centuries. They may simply need to be repackaged and applied to a contemporary culture.

Consider that one of the best-selling management books of the last decade was *The Leadership Secrets of Attila the Hun.* Author Wess Roberts reached back into the past and brought someone to life who had been relegated to history as a barbaric tyrant. But Attila's principles, used so long ago to motivate and mobilize his motley forces into a nation of spirited Huns, are accurate and applicable to our world today.

Or consider the marketing success of *The Art of War* by the ancient Chinese warrior Sun Tzu. The strategies and management principles of this warrior-philosopher of twenty-five hundred years ago have found their way into the briefcases and "war rooms" of thousands of business executives in the United States over the last decade.

Once again, from out of the past, comes a timeless document, a piece of personal correspondence, written by a people strategist to a wealthy entrepreneur almost two thousand years ago. It contains only a few sentences, and yet, it is the most eloquent case study in building positive, productive relationships to be found anywhere. This ancient document, known as Philemon, is preserved in the New Testament for all posterity. Philemon was a very successful landowner and businessman in the first-century city of Colosse. This letter, which bears his name, primarily involves two other people—Paul and a man named Onesimus.

Paul, the author of the letter, was actually writing from a prison in Rome where he was incarcerated for his allegiance to a new and growing movement called Christianity. Onesimus was, in essence, a contractual employee of the more influential and wealthy Philemon.

The letter reveals the relationships between the three individuals, and it is a gold mine of lessons on how to get along with others. Onesimus broke his contract with Philemon and left town. By the strangest circumstances, he made his way to Rome, was arrested, and found himself in prison with Paul.

Even more coincidentally, Paul was a personal friend of Philemon and had, in fact, won him to Christ on a previous visit to Colosse. In the constant presence of this warm and winsome people person, Onesimus came to see the error of his ways, and he was transformed through his faith in Christ. The proof was that, after his release from jail, he planned to return to Colosse, tell Philemon how sorry he was, and try to make restitution.

Paul wrote this letter to Philemon to pave the way for Onesimus's return. It is a marvelous blueprint for building positive, fruitful relationships.

Life is made up of relationships. We must deal with people every day, and the quality of these relationships is crucial to everyone's happiness and well-being. Perhaps today you will need to complain to a landlord or to cope with a problem in your social life. Husbands and wives want to understand each other; teachers are always trying to translate truth to their students; athletes long to please their coaches.

Some of us have experienced great heartache or have caused great heartache because we have never learned how to relate to others in a positive and effective way.

The intent of both this book and the content of Philemon's letter is not just how to make friends but how to keep them in long-term, mutually beneficial relationships.

Let's open this timeless piece of personal correspondence, look over Philemon's shoulder, so to speak, and discover some well-worn and lasting secrets in the art of connecting with others.

SECTION I

The Art
of Connecting

*Paul, a prisoner of Christ Jesus, and Timothy our
brother, to Philemon our beloved friend and fellow la-
borer, to the beloved Apphia, Archippus our fellow soldier, and to the church in your house: Grace to you and
peace from God our Father and the Lord Jesus Christ.*
—Philemon 1–3

CHAPTER ONE

THE
SOURCE

I HAVE ALWAYS BEEN an early riser. It doesn't matter whether I go to bed early or late, rested or worn out; I am automatically wide awake at five minutes until six every morning. You can set your watch by it.

Recently, I flew from Fort Lauderdale to the West Coast where I was to speak at a convention in the San Francisco Bay area. Sure enough, I awoke the following morning at 5:55 A.M.

The only problem was that I was still on East Coast time. The little red numerals on the clock radio in my hotel room greeted me with 2:55 A.M.! I tried my best to go back to sleep, to no avail. Finally, I reached for the television remote control and flicked on the tube.

It doesn't matter where you are in America or what time of the day or night it might be, there are always two things you can get on television: world championship wrestling and religious programming. And there they were in living color at three in the morning in Oakland. (And by the way, the world is asking the same question about them both—"Is it real, or is it fake?")

Honestly, I could not take either one at that hour, so I got up and went to a desk by the window to work on some projects in my briefcase. I reached for the switch on the desk lamp and turned it on, but nothing happened. So I began a little detective work. I came to the brilliant conclusion that the lamp had only three possible points of connection.

First, I looked at the source. It was plugged in. Next, I checked the switch. It was turned on. There was only one other possibility: the socket. Bingo! The bulb was not screwed down tightly into the socket. I gave it a couple of turns, and there was light.

Life is a lot like that lamp. Add up all our relationships and they boil down to three dimensions.

First, we have a relationship with God. This is the upward connection, or the Source. We have an innate longing to connect with the Source, to be plugged in to the only power that can give our lives meaning.

Second, we have a relationship with ourselves. This is the inward connection, the switch. To be happy and effective in life, we must have the proper self-respect and self-love.

Finally, we have relationships with others, in the home, the office, and the social arena. This is the outward connection, or the socket. To light up the lives of those around us, we need to be in right relationship with ourselves, with others, and with God. I like to call it the art of connecting.

The Source, the Switch, and the Socket

Two thousand years ago, Paul of Tarsus took these principles of relationships and cleverly used them in his greeting to Philemon. Paul was plugged in to an unlimited outside power supply, the Source. He was also connected at the switch; he possessed self-respect and self-confidence. Finally, he was connected at the socket; his relationships were solid and secure. The result of being plugged in and turned on was that when he touched the lives of others, he brought a light that brightened their road and had a way of lightening their load at the same time.

Let's take these three life-building principles and examine them one at a time, starting with the most important relationship of all: the Source.

Our Eternal Connection

In Paul's first words to Philemon, "Grace to you and peace from God our Father" (v. 3), he reveals much about his own connection with the Source. Although we tend to scan right past the words *grace* and *peace*, they give a beautiful description of our new status with God. We have His undeserved favor, love, and protection, and we are at peace with Him. We did nothing to deserve these gifts, but we are grateful receivers.

Paul knew what an enemy of God he had been. He understood something of the enormity of his sin, and he marveled at the place to which God had brought him. He knew he was not deserving of this, just as Onesimus was not deserving of clemency from Philemon.

How many of us, I wonder, spend much time thinking about the depth of God's grace and the peace that it brings to us? Do we really understand the all-encompassing nature of His love and forgiveness? In his book *The Grace Awakening*, Chuck Swindoll emphasizes this amazing truth about grace:

It is absolutely and totally free. You will never be asked to pay it back. You couldn't even if you tried. Most of us have trouble with that thought, because we work for everything we get. As the old saying goes, "There ain't no free lunch." But in this case, grace comes to us free and clear, no strings attached. We should not even try to repay it; to do so is insulting.[1]

But does this grace we have been given affect the way we treat one another? Swindoll continues:

My plea is that we not limit it to Him. We, too, can learn to be just as gracious as He. And since we can, we must . . . not only in our words and in great acts of compassion and understanding but in small ways as well.

Sir Edward C. Burne-Jones, the prominent nineteenth-century English artist, went to tea at the home of his daughter. As a special treat his little granddaughter was allowed to come to the table; she misbehaved, and her mother made her stand in the corner with her face to the wall. Sir Edward, a well-trained grandfather, did not interfere with his grandchild's training, but next morning he arrived at his daughter's home with paints and palette. He went to the wall where the little girl had been forced to stand, and there he painted pictures—a kitten chasing its tail; lambs in a field; goldfish swimming. He decorated the wall on both sides of that corner with paintings for his granddaughter's delight. If she had to stand in the corner again, at least she would have something to look at.

And so it is with our Lord. When we do the things we should not, He may administer discipline, sometimes quite severely, but He never turns His back. . . . He doesn't send His child to hell! Neither do we fall from grace and get slammed behind the iron bars of the Law. He deals with His own in grace . . . beautiful, charming, unmerited favor.[2]

Paul, I'm convinced, had great appreciation and gratitude for the grace God had given him. And in his first words of greeting, he wished that same sense of grace and peace on Philemon. It is the ultimate encouragement from one brother in Christ to another.

God as Father

To indicate his own relationship with God, Paul refers to God as *patros*, the Greek word for "father." He saw himself in a Father-and-son relationship with the Source of power. Paul had the peace and confidence that come from being a member of the family, from being an heir.

The same word *patros* is used to describe the father in the story of the prodigal son. When the boy asked for his inheritance prematurely, left his responsibilities, and went off to indulge himself, his father didn't have to release him. He could have blackmailed him with the inheritance money. He could have simply refused his son. But he respected the boy's freedom and let him go, hoping all the while for his change of heart.

It didn't take the son long to lose it all, along with his dignity and self-respect. What had promised to be a good time brought nothing but disappointment, humiliation, and unemployment lines.

The story has a happy ending, though. The boy decided to get up and go home, not knowing what his father would say or do. I think the outcome surprised him.

The same dad who had earlier said, "I release you," now said, "I receive you. And what is more, I celebrate your return as my son." When the boy returned with a repentant heart, the father received him with open arms and rewarded him for finally doing what was right (Luke 15:11–32). All of that is wrapped up in this word *patros* or "father," which Paul uses to describe his own connection with the Source in his letter to Philemon.

Father. That is a tough word for some people. In fact, for many it is the word at the root of many unresolved problems in relationships. Low self-esteem due to a poor relationship with a dad can make it very difficult to relate successfully to others.

Paul may have experienced strong disapproval from his own father; perhaps he even knew what complete rejection felt like. His elite education, his membership in the Sanhedrin, and his status in Jewish society certainly would have been gratifying to his father. When he gave up everything for Christ's cause, we can only imagine what it might have done to his relationship with a proud Jewish dad.

But Paul is not talking about an earthly father here. He is visualizing a relationship with the perfect Father, the Source of eternal peace and power, who accepts us just as we are.

Knowing we're accepted enables us to accept ourselves and others. Knowing He puts everything we need at our disposal frees us to give generously to others of our time, our resources, and our love. We no longer have to wonder where we stand with Him.

Contrast this sense of confidence and peace with the feelings of Richard, who works for a large family-owned dairy. Richard has driven a milk delivery truck for the past two years, but he has set his sights on bigger things—being a sales manager. When someone asks him why, his answer is quick: "Because of the higher salary! I'd be making a third more money than I am now, and besides, sales managers get more respect."

So, much of Richard's time and energy is devoted to how he can get ahead. At the same time, he tries to fulfill his present responsibilities so that he won't get fired. "I don't think I'm in danger of being fired," he asserts. "But you never know. I just try to keep my bases covered." If the truth were known, Richard isn't in danger of losing his job, but his lack of relationship with the kindhearted owner leaves him with a tremendous sense of insecurity.

Compare Richard with Vance, the son of the owner and grandson of the dairy's founder. He knows the heavy responsibility he will carry one day as head of the company. But he is relaxed, and there is a spring in his step as he goes about his work. Why? He is the son. The heir. He doesn't worry about being fired, but he still works harder than almost anyone because his heart is in the business. The boss is his father, who loves him and wants to give him everything he owns.

Knowing all this colors everything Vance thinks and everything he does. One day he ran into a secretary in the hallway. She had just spilled a cartridge of copier ink, and she was almost in tears as she tried to clean it up while several employees passed by, unknowingly tracking it with them.

Vance didn't think twice. "Here, let me help you," he offered. And he cleaned it up. No job is too menial for someone who has the company's best interests at heart.

When it comes to your relationship with God, do you see yourself as a Richard, someone who is afraid of messing up and getting fired? Are you not quite sure where you stand? Is it hard to make time for others because you are looking out for your own interests and advancement?

Or are you a Vance? You're sure where you stand in your Father's mind and heart, and you're sure of your future with Him. Are you completely devoted to Him out of gratitude for what He gives you? Are the people He cares about important to you?

Our heavenly Father releases us to be the unique people that we were created to be. He now expects us not to live selfishly for ourselves, but for others. He respects us, and what's more, He trusts us! He trusts us with the most important things to Him—people. And if we abuse this trust, He releases us, but He doesn't give up. The very moment we are ready to come back to Him, He receives us with open arms and allows us to start all over again.

He will become Father and a source of strength to all who come to Him, especially those of us who might not have had a positive experience with an earthly father. Psalm 27:10 addresses this situation: "When my father and my mother forsake me,/ Then the LORD will take care of me."

The eternal connection, touching the Source, begins when we, like Paul, see God as our Father, and we become His sons and daughters through our relationship with Christ.

God As Lord

Paul continues in his greeting to Philemon saying, "Grace to you and peace from God our Father *and the Lord Jesus Christ*" (v. 3, emphasis mine). With these words he brings in the one requirement for his relationship with the Source of his power.

Again, writing in Greek, he gives his source the name *kurios*, which is translated into English as "Lord." He sees his source not only as Father but also as Lord. He views himself as a son and a servant.

Remember, he is writing this letter on relationships to Philemon in regard to his relationship with a former servant/employee by the name of Onesimus. With these words Paul is subtly showing Philemon that we are all sons and daughters and servants of our God, the Source.

In his letter to the Colossians, Philemon's home church, Paul wrote, "Masters, give your bondservants what is just and fair, knowing that you also have a Master in heaven" (Col. 4:1). He was emphasizing this same truth to Philemon. Though God is our Father, He is also our Lord. This fact is important to remember if we are to keep our relationship with God and others in proper perspective.

God As Savior

Paul next goes a step further by referring to his source of power as a promised One, a Savior. In the letter, he calls Him *Christos*, which we translate "Christ." For Paul, a learned and aristocratic Jew, he found his source in the promised Messiah, for whom the world had been waiting.

Throughout his life, Paul had celebrated that high and holy Day of Atonement, Yom Kippur. In Hebrew, *Yom Kippur* means "the day of covering." On Yom Kippur, the sins of the previous year were covered by a blood sacrifice.

Today, our Jewish friends have abandoned their blood sacrifices, and they seek their "covering" through *Mitzvot* (good works). Paul, in referring to his source as *Christos*, identifies Him as the promised One who came to become a covering for all our faults and failures and to bring us purpose, peace, and a positive self-image.

This can be illustrated with a mental trip back to my hotel in Oakland, mentioned earlier. When it was time to check out of the hotel I did not pay cash. Instead, I used a credit card, which has no value in and of itself. It is simply a piece of plastic. But the hotel clerk accepted my credit card as if it were cash.

Why did she do that? It was a forerunner of the true payment that was sure to follow. The actual payment came a few weeks later when I received my statement in the mail and paid my bill. Until then the credit card simply covered the purchase.

In the same way, the old covenant between God and people, with its sacrificial system, covered the faults and failures of those who believed in the promised One to come. And He came! He made the final payment for our covering with the sacrifice of His own life on a Roman cross of execution.

Because of this, our relationship with the Father has been purchased and secured. Paul saw his source as Father and himself as a valued member of the family. Paul's debt to God was covered, and because he was secure, he was free to attend to the business at hand of helping people.

When we see ourselves as children of a loving Father, everything changes. We know where we stand with Him. We are secure, and we are free to go about our lives in the peace and confidence that He offers. It is a marvelous way to live!

CHAPTER TWO

THE
SWITCH

GOOD INTERPERSONAL RELATION-
SHIPS develop from the inside out. They
have not only an eternal connection but
also an internal one. Like a lamp that gives light, they are
plugged in at the Source and turned on at the switch.

The problem with so many interpersonal relationships is a
breakdown at one of these points of connection. Some people
have a very difficult time relating to others, primarily because
they do not feel good about themselves. Others have such low
self-image and such fear of rejection that they never make contact
with others, and the light that could mean so much to so many
is never turned on.

Bill is a good example. He works ten hours a day, driving a
truck for a delivery company. When he comes home to his wife
and daughter, he retreats to the garage where he works on an old
car. When the weekend arrives, he hitches his fishing boat to the
truck and heads for the lake, many times spending Saturday and
Sunday away from home.

On the surface, Bill's family doesn't seem to care that he
remains distant emotionally and physically. That is probably

because even when he is around, he is withdrawn and gruff. His fuse is as short as they come, and any transgression sets him off. Invariably, when he loses his temper, he retreats to his garage once again, his safe haven from the pressures of the world and its problems.

We all feel sorry for people like Bill. We want to help, but we often don't know how. They work so hard at keeping their distance that we are unable to befriend them in any meaningful way. All the while, they retreat further and further into a world of loneliness and isolation.

Bill has problems accepting himself, and those problems make it difficult for him to accept others, including his family. His poor self-image stands as a barrier to developing deep, personal relationships with other people. And until he learns to accept and love himself, regardless of his inevitable flaws and shortcomings, he will never be fully connected with others.

The Problem of Self-Rejection

Many of us reject others in our relationships because we have such a hard time accepting ourselves. When we suffer from self-rejection, we are prone to project our feelings of low self-worth onto others, resulting in the destruction of our relationships.

How does it work on a practical level? If I am insecure and have little self-confidence, I usually become threatened by others and project this attitude onto them. If I live in self-pity, I project a martyr's complex, always portraying myself as the innocent victim. If I am unethical and have little self-respect, I become suspicious of others, thinking that they are out to cheat me. When I am critical of myself, I instinctively become critical of others.

Self-rejection does that to us. It affects every feeling and emotion we have. And it affects every one of our relationships.

But what are some of the root causes of self-rejection? We can look to several places for the answer.

Some blame their relational failures on their heredity. They say, "I lose my temper because my dad did. It's in my DNA. I inherited it." In some senses, they may not be far from wrong. Though I don't believe self-rejection can be inherited, certain personality traits are definitely passed down through the genes. It is possible to be born with a propensity toward self-rejection; a melancholy personality might be a good candidate.

But self-rejection more likely results from how we were raised as children. Child abuse, whether physical or emotional, is at the root of many low self-images. Some of us began life with emotionally ill parents who never touched us or showed us love or who, perhaps, demanded more than we could ever deliver.

Self-rejection can also arise out of the premium our society places on beauty. Our culture tells us in a thousand ways that self-image is built around being beautiful, and many of us have bought into that lie.

Since so much value is placed on good looks, many reject themselves because they are not pretty or handsome enough. But anyone who tries to find self-worth in outward appearance is headed for trouble because sags and wrinkles are just around the corner for all of us.

Lack of superior intelligence can cause a person to feel insecure. In our society, highly intelligent people get the best salaries, the biggest offices, and the highest respect. Woe to the person with a two-digit IQ in a world where such premium is placed on mental ability. Feeling unintelligent is never fun, and it is usually a major catalyst for self-rejection.

Whatever the cause, self-rejection is a major barrier to connecting with others in a meaningful way. And it robs relationships of so much potential joy and fulfillment.

Selfishness or Self-Respect?

What is a healthy self-image? I am not referring to self-centeredness, self-exaltation, or selfishness. A healthy self-image has to do with accepting and respecting oneself. It is seeing ourselves as God sees us.

If we know anything about God, we should view ourselves highly, having been made in His image and having been entrusted with His creation (Gen. 1:26). In addition to this, we've been rescued from a terrible fate at an extremely high price. Knowing how much God loves us frees us to love ourselves and others as well.

Poor self-image is at the very core of society's ills. Every day we read in our newspapers about problems brought on by such things as drug addiction, violence, prostitution, and other social disorders. These are most often the fruits of a much deeper root of low self-respect.

Large segments of a generation of young people have now been raised with little self-esteem, so it is no surprise when they view themselves in such a low fashion that disastrous results occur.

It is possible to change the way we feel about ourselves, but meaningful, lasting change can come only from the Source of our very lives, from a solid connection with Him, and from the realization of how important we are to Him.

A New View of You

We see this change in the life of Gideon, one of the great judges of ancient Israel. When first commissioned to save his country from the Midianites, Gideon replied, "O my Lord, how can I save Israel? Indeed my clan is the weakest in Manasseh, and I am the least in my father's house" (Judg. 6:15).

Gideon started out with a poor self-image and a poor connection with the Source of his strength and success, but he ended up a conqueror with the respect of the whole country. He accepted God's kindness and patient demonstrations of faithfulness, and he became courageous and faithful in the face of daunting circumstances.

Contrast Gideon's life with that of Saul, Israel's first king. At the outset, Saul seemed to have almost everything going for him. He was from a good family. His father, Kish, was described as "a man of standing" (1 Sam. 9:1 NIV). Saul was described as "a choice and handsome son. . . . There was not a more handsome person than he among the children of Israel. From his shoulders upward he was taller than any of the people" (1 Sam. 9:2).

When Samuel anointed him king over Israel, he voiced some powerful prophecies about Saul's future, including the words, "The Spirit of the LORD will come upon you in power, and you will prophesy . . . and you will be changed into a different person" (1 Sam. 10:6 NIV).

Who of us hasn't at one time or another wanted to be changed like this? Have our friends and family noticed a change in us like Saul's friends did in him? "And it happened, when all who knew him formerly saw that he indeed prophesied among the prophets, that the people said to one another, 'What is this that has come upon the son of Kish? Is Saul also among the prophets?'" (1 Sam. 10:11).

And yet the story has an unhappy ending. Saul did not remain connected with the Source. He did not face his calling and commission as king with dignity and courage. Saul's low self-esteem and cowardice manifested themselves embarrassingly at the moment he was to be made king in the presence of all the Israelites. In fact, he was nowhere to be found, having hidden himself among the baggage. It took the Lord's guidance to Samuel to ferret him out.

Saul's reign was an almost unbroken display of disobedience and lack of trust in the Lord. He was not properly plugged in to the Source, and consequently, he felt poorly about himself and his relationships with others. God offers us a powerful and meaningful life in His presence, but we must be willing to sustain the connection.

Changing Our Attitudes by Changing Our Actions

Developing our relationships from the inside out is a process in which "being comes before doing," for our circumstances are largely determined by who we are and what we do.

For example, if you want to have a more fulfilling marriage, be a more considerate husband or wife. Begin with yourself. If you want to have a more cooperative teenager, be a more consistent, understanding, and loving parent. If you want your mom or dad to be more fair with you, be the kind of son or daughter you ought to be. Dust off those old words about honoring and obeying your parents. If you want to have greater opportunity for advancement in the workplace, be the hardest working, most efficient, and most pleasant and cooperative worker in the office. In short, if you want to have a true friend, be a true friend.

Paul realized that to have Philemon as a friend, he must first be a friend to Philemon. And his friendship sprang from the heart, not from ulterior motives.

A Prisoner of Love

In his own words, Paul refers to himself as a "prisoner of Jesus Christ" (v. 9), and in so doing, he reveals much about his connection with himself. As he penned these words in Greek, he chose an interesting word (*desmios*) to describe himself as a prisoner.

It is of note that in writing to Philemon, he does not say he is a "prisoner of Rome." Indeed, he was, at the time of his writing, an actual prisoner of Nero and the Roman Empire. They are the ones who had incarcerated him. They kept watch over him. But they had only a small part in the drama.

In actuality, Paul saw himself first and foremost as a "prisoner of Jesus Christ." He was not there by accident. His life had been placed in God's care and control, and though the Romans thought that he was their prisoner, he knew better.

Don't misunderstand what Paul is saying about himself here. This is no self-effacing statement reflecting a low self-image. He does not refer to himself as a prisoner "for" Jesus Christ; he is a prisoner "of" Jesus Christ, indicating he is one whom the Source of power has brought under His authority.

Every one of us is a prisoner of someone or something. Some are prisoners of our own passion. Others are prisoners of our popularity. Still others are held captive by pride. Some are imprisoned by success, and others by a particular person. How much better, though, to be a prisoner of the Source of all things. True self-worth and self-respect are found in being a "prisoner of Jesus Christ."

There is a sense in which all the creation should see itself as "prisoner" of the Creator. Being held captive by His love has a liberating effect on our own self-image.

We see this principle often in romantic relationships. When Sharon fell in love, her special new man eclipsed almost everything else. She would do anything for John; nothing was too much trouble. Most dramatically of all, her face seemed to change. It was lit with the wonderful reality of her relationship with him. And his deep feelings for her gave her a sense of security that made her more others-centered than she'd been in the past.

When we are captivated by Christ's love for us, it changes our actions, our thoughts, our motives, and even our faces.

Gaining Through Giving Up

A healthy self-image does not come from a pseudo, pumped up mental attitude. It results from being connected with the Source to the extent that we realize how valuable we are to Him. Our Creator has gone out of His way to give us a sense of how much we mean to Him.

In John 15:15, Jesus said, "No longer do I call you servants, for a servant does not know what his master is doing; but I have called you friends, for all things that I heard from My Father I have made known to you."

We read in Zephaniah 3:17:

> *The LORD your God in your midst,*
> *The Mighty One, will save;*

He will rejoice over you with gladness,
He will quiet you with His love,
He will rejoice over you with singing.

Do you know anyone who sings love songs about you? Well, God does!

This idea of losing ourselves in the Source in order to really find ourselves is in diametric opposition to most worldviews today. That is why so many people are living such confused and complicated lives. Many have bought into the superficial and deceptive message of New Age awareness in their quest to "find themselves."

When I speak of being in touch with the self or being connected with the self, I am not referring to a New Age concept of self-improvement or self-awareness. Quite the contrary! Jesus of Nazareth put it like this: "He who finds his life will lose it, and he who loses his life for My sake will find it" (Matt. 10:39).

There is only one way to find ourselves, and many miss it because it is paradoxical. We find ourselves when we submit to what God wants for us and from us. When we die to ourselves and live for Him, we have discovered true fulfillment.

The Source of Our Self-Image

Paul was the single most successful people strategist of his day, and one of the reasons was his self-confidence. He felt good about himself. He had purpose in life and a spirit of conquest about him. He was positively connected with himself. Why? Because of his relationship with the Source. He was plugged in to power and turned on so that this supernatural winsomeness and warmth flowed into him and through him into the lives of people he knew. His mission pulsated with power until its completion.

Strength and identity come from one's source. If we are connected only with the self, if the self is our source, then we have nothing more than a shallow self-awareness and must constantly be pumping ourselves up like some old-fashioned surface pump well behind a farmhouse.

Some people today go from one self-help guru to the next, one tape to the next, one book to the next, one seminar to the next. Pump, pump, pump. But when we find our proper self-image at our Source, it is like an artesian well. You do not have to pump an artesian well. You just turn it on, and it flows because it is dug deep into the ground and has tapped into an underground river as its source.

The Source of Our Confidence

The prophet Isaiah records a moving story in his Old Testament book about the moment he was given his life commission from God. It was the moment he came face to face with the Source of his power.

It was in the year that King Uzziah died, and Isaiah was given a vision of heaven:

> I saw the Lord sitting on a throne, high and lifted up,
> and the train of His robe filled the temple. Above it
> stood seraphim. . . . And one cried to another and said:
> "Holy, holy, holy is the LORD of hosts;
> The whole earth is full of His glory!"

*And the posts of the door were shaken by the voice of him
who cried out, and the house was filled with smoke.
(Isa. 6:1–4)*

Isaiah saw just a glimpse of the glory of God. And when he
did, he was devastated by his own sinfulness:

*Woe is me, for I am undone!
Because I am a man of unclean lips,
And I dwell in the midst of a people of unclean lips;
For my eyes have seen the King,
The LORD of hosts. (6:5)*

Just then, something extraordinary happened:

*Then one of the seraphim flew to me, having in his hand
a live coal which he had taken with the tongs from the al-
tar. And he touched my mouth with it, and said:
"Behold, this has touched your lips;
Your iniquity is taken away,
And your sin purged." (6:6–7)*

In a moment, Isaiah was forgiven of his sins. For the first
time in his life, he felt the joy of God's redemption.

That was when God called him to the work of a prophet.

"Whom shall I send?" God asked. "And who will go for Us?"

Isaiah's immediate and grateful response was a confident
"Here am I! Send me" (6:8).

When we recognize what God has done for us, and when we
accept the friendship that He offers, we gain the confidence and

the courage to go forward with renewed excitement and exuberance in life. We want to try things we never dreamed we'd be able to accomplish.

In subsequent letters to other individuals, Paul said such things as "I can do all things through Christ who strengthens me" (Phil. 4:13). In a letter to his friends in Rome, he reminded them that "we are more than conquerors through Him who loved us" (Rom. 8:37).

How could he make such statements? He was connected at the Source, and thus, he was confident in the self. He lost his life in the love of his Source, and consequently, he found it. It changed his life and his eternal destiny.

In Paul's earlier years, he wrote some friends in Galatia in A.D. 49 and referred to himself as "an apostle." I can see him now as he sat smugly in his chair and penned those words. Five or six years later he wrote to the church in Corinth and referred to himself as "the least of the apostles."

Then in A.D. 60, he referred to himself as "less than the least of all God's people." A year or so after that, he wrote our letter to Philemon, referring to himself as "a prisoner of Jesus Christ." And finally, near the end of his life, he penned a moving letter to his young associate Timothy, and he called himself the "chief" of sinners (1 Tim. 1:15).

Most of the world would not recognize this as much of a proper self-image, but most of the world does not look beyond the surface. The more this man lost his life in the love of his source of strength, the more he found it.

Seeing Ourselves Through God's Eyes

Much of our low self-esteem comes from the influences of

those around us. In some cases it has been our parents, and in other cases our peers. But what is most important in recovering damaged emotions and low self-esteem is not what others think about us but what God, the ultimate Source of all power, thinks about us. And He loves us . . . just as we are!

When we, through faith, become His children He says the same thing of each of us He said of His own Son: "This is My beloved Son, in whom I am well pleased" (Matt. 3:17). God's Son did not leave His throne to come down to die for individuals of no worth or little value. We are indescribably valuable to Him. And when this realization reaches the core of our beings, it will change our self-images and our lives.

Jeff is a dramatic illustration of this. He started life with several strikes against him: born into a family who didn't know God, he was raised by parents who were physically there but didn't provide the guidance he needed. To top it all off, he was rather homely!

Things went from bad to worse as Jeff grew up. Finally, he landed in prison at age eighteen, with his self-esteem at an all-time low. While incarcerated, he came to know Christ as a result of a ministry to the men in that prison. He came to have a sense of worth and direction that he could not have imagined just a short time earlier.

After he was released, he enrolled in a Christian college and earned a degree in Bible, then a master's in missions. The transformation was amazing. Jeff knew the depth to which he had fallen, and he knew how far God had reached to pick him up. His appreciation and love for Christ radiated from everything he did, giving him confidence that stood out on the campus.

Jeff's confidence made him a natural leader. He inspired many other students to do foreign mission work, and he led several teams overseas. Even Jeff's face shone with the light that only the Source can give, and many women vied for his attention. Today, he serves the Lord in Africa, in the face of significant personal hardship.

When Moses, the ancient Jewish leader, was singled out to become the emancipator of his people he responded with a question: "Who am I?" (Ex. 3:11). No question could come any closer to the heart of the matter. Moses had extremely low confidence and self-esteem, but God had a job for him and believed in him.

When Moses took the challenge that God had given him, when he obeyed, God took him by the hand and gave him the confidence and ability to do everything required of him.

Let's not insult God's creation by expecting less of ourselves than He does! I am a spirit made in the image of God Himself, and the only way to really touch myself is to know God through His Son Jesus Christ, who is Himself the "express image" of the Father.

What is the bottom line in successful relationships with others? We will never have true self-worth until we see how valuable we are to the Father and become connected with the Source of life Himself.

CHAPTER THREE

THE SOCKET

NOT LONG AFTER JACK BENNY died, his longtime friend and partner, George Burns, was interviewed on television. "Jack and I had a wonderful friendship for nearly fifty-five years," he said. "Jack never walked out on me when I sang a song, and I never walked out on him when he played the violin. We laughed together, we played together, we worked together, we ate together. I suppose that for many of those years we talked every single day."[1]

We all long for those kinds of relationships, don't we? We want friends who understand us, who enjoy being with us. We want friends who will laugh at our jokes, remember our birthdays, cry with us when we're sad, and stick by us when all others have left. We want someone who will always be there for us, no matter what.

God wired us for relationships, and we can't exist without them. Small babies die without loving touch. Children are emotionally scarred for life in the absence of a loving parental relationship. It is said that bachelors, on the whole, don't live as long as married men, and even married men who kiss their wives before leaving the house have fewer accidents than those who don't!

"Friendships . . . ," writes Alan McGinnis,

". . . spill over onto the other important relationships of life. People with no friends usually have a diminished capacity for sustaining *any* kind of love. They tend to go through a succession of marriages, be estranged from various family members, and have trouble getting along at work. On the other hand, those who learn how to love their friends tend to make long and fulfilling marriages, get along well with the people at work, and enjoy their children."[2]

We are made to relate positively with one another. We are created for companionship, for deep, meaningful friendships with others.

Back in the beginning of creation, a phrase was repeated over and over. The Creator paused at the conclusion of each part of His handiwork to say, "That's good!" He said it about the skies, the land, the sea, the vegetation, the animals, and all His creation. Until He made a man. And soon His words were, "Not good!" He said, "It is not good that man should be alone" (Gen. 2:18). So God made Adam a companion, someone to help, encourage, and even confront him when necessary.

We are social beings who, by our very nature, are made to interact and relate with one another. Like a lamp, though, we can fulfill our purpose only when we are connected with the Source. His power begins to flow through us and then out of us, touching others and lighting their way. Romans 14:19 urges us, "Therefore let us pursue the things which make for peace and the things by which one may edify another."

In the salutation to his letter to Philemon, Paul begins by saying, "To Philemon our dear friend and fellow worker, to Apphia our sister, to Archippus our fellow soldier and to the church that meets in your home" (vv. 1–2 NIV). Because Paul was properly connected with God and with himself, he related to others in four ways. He sees these external relationships as family, friends, fellow workers, and fellow soldiers.

Seeing Others As Family

First, we need to see one another as family. Paul did. And that was one of the secrets to his success. He built a family consciousness and cohesiveness with those who were in his inner circle. He spoke of his associate, Timothy, as a "brother" and referred to Apphia (most likely Philemon's wife) as a "sister." A careful reading of the letter reveals the constant repetition of the personal pronoun *our*—"our brother . . . our dear friend . . . our fellow worker . . . our sister . . . our fellow soldier." That was not by accident. Building a spirit of community and camaraderie is vital in our relationships.

But how can we be a community in an age of *self*-involvement and in a culture that praises rugged individualism? By remembering whose we are and what He has done for us.

The early church described in the book of Acts is probably the most dramatic account of what can happen to people when they have internalized Christ's sacrifice for them. Because that group of people realized that they had been bought by Christ, that He owned them and all that they had, pride and selfishness fell by the wayside. They were replaced by sensitivity to the needs of others and a willingness to meet those needs in whatever ways they could. True friendships are really family affairs.

I like the way Doug Fagerstrom and James Carlson describe what community life should be like in a church family:

> One single adult in our church commented, "I just need to know that I can walk into room 132 every Sunday morning and know that my friends will be there and I will be fed from God's Word and encouraged to hang in there. . . ." Another single said after a one-year, short-term missions project, "It is so good to be home." She was not referring to the city of Grand Rapids, nor to her parents' house. She meant the family of believers who had supported, prayed for, and sent her overseas. . . . As she opened the "family photo album" she told through tears how she had missed the fellowship, music, love, care, and ministry outreach to others through a community of believers in the local church. After a few more tears, she went off encouraged to obey her call back to the mission field. This is how the home works. This is what it can provide. This *is* the family of God.[3]

Seeing Others As Friends

Following Paul's example, we need to see one another as friends as well as family. He addresses Philemon at the outset with much affection and calls him a "dear friend." Genuine friendship is like a beautiful flower. Our relationship with others is the fruit. Our relationship with ourselves is the shoot. Our relationship with God, the Source, is the root.

Toward the end of His earthly ministry, Jesus gave this life-changing message to His disciples: "A new commandment

I give to you, that you love one another; as I have loved you, that you also love one another. By this all will know that you are My disciples, if you have love for one another" (John 13:34–35).

The disciples had spent three years seeing Christ's love in action. Their love for one another would be modeled on His love for them and would draw an unbelieving world to God.

The world is still watching to see how we treat one another and to see if we love our brothers and sisters in Christ. They want to know if this love we profess is genuine and if it includes them.

Hussein was one of the people watching and taking mental notes. He grew up in the Iranian capital of Tehran. His world revolved around his family, the teachings of the Koran, and his fervent desire to immigrate to the United States.

At last, Hussein's dream came true. After a long-awaited permission to study in America was granted, his plane touched down one hot August day in a small Texas city.

Hussein knew no one at first. He struggled to settle into a community whose language and customs were foreign to him. In time, though, he was befriended by several believers in the community. Their love for one another was a new, refreshing experience for the stranger. Their love for him was bewildering, yet irresistible. In time, through the friendship, prayers, and fasting for the soul of the young man, he became a believer.

Seeing Others As Fellow Workers

Paul referred to Philemon not only as a dear friend but also as a "fellow worker." As he penned his letter in Greek, he chose *synergos* to describe this relationship with his friend. It is a compound word that literally means to "work with." We get the

English words *synergism* and *synergy* from this Greek word. In more common terms, synergism simply means that the whole is greater than the sum of the parts.

Two pencils can illustrate this amazing truth. If you hold them together and try to break them, it takes a good deal more strength than would be needed to break each individually. With synergism, one plus one does not necessarily equal two. It equals three or more.

In using this word that means "fellow worker," Paul is showing us how much we really do need one another. This dynamic power in interpersonal relationships is illustrated in the Bible when it says, "Five of you shall chase a hundred, and a hundred of you shall put ten thousand to flight; / your enemies shall fall by the sword before you" (Lev. 26:8). This is synergism in action.

Jesus once said, "If two of you agree on earth concerning anything that they ask, it will be done for them by My Father in heaven" (Matt. 18:19).

The wisest man who ever lived, King Solomon, put it like this:

> *Two are better than one,*
> *Because they have a good reward for their labor.*
> *For if they fall, one will lift up his companion.*
> *But woe to him who is alone when he falls,*
> *For he has no one to help him up.*
> *Again, if two lie down together, they will keep warm;*
> *But how can one be warm alone?*
> *Though one may be overpowered by another,*
>   *two can withstand him.*
> *And a threefold cord is not quickly broken. (Ecc. 4:9–12)*

Bob had spent many years as a missionary to Austria. But he and his family needed help, and just as crucially, they needed the encouragement that friendship with fellow workers could provide. One day he paid a visit to Ed, an acquaintance and longtime minister in the United States.

"Ed, we need you and Jean over there," he told him. "You understand the culture, you speak the language, and you even like the food! Come over and help us!"

It did work out for Ed and Jean to go, and in that ministry, the families began a friendship that has lasted for over twenty years.

When Christ sent out disciples to the surrounding areas, He sent them two by two. That was no coincidence. He knows we need encouragement, friendship, and even accountability.

Paul was a people person, and he realized the importance of working together with others toward a common goal. Effective interpersonal relationships are the result not of competition but of cooperation. "Fellow workers" share each other's dreams, work together in unity toward the same goal, and share in each other's victories as though they were their own.

Much is accomplished when two people work together synergistically. Synergism takes place when a father and a mother connect in parenting. This is a vital principle in our effort to raise positive kids in a negative world. If parents are not united in discipline, significant damage can be done to the upbringing of a child. However, when they connect and stand together, when one speaks and acts in unison with the other, the child soon gets the message, and powerful and positive results take place.

Synergism happens when a teacher and a student connect on

an assignment. They become "fellow workers," and learning takes place. It occurs when members of a project team brainstorm together, and new ideas and plans begin to take shape. The epitome of synergism takes place when a bride and a groom leave the wedding altar to become one.

Working together for a common good is an indispensable principle in managing and maintaining productive relationships with others.

Seeing Others As Fellow Soldiers

Paul goes a step further in his discussion of relationships by referring in his letter to Philemon's son, Archippus, as a "fellow soldier." He uses a very descriptive Greek word, *sustratiootees*, which carries with it the connotation of a fellow combatant, a comrade in arms, one who faced the same dangers and fought in the same foxhole in the same conflict. As believers who are connected to the same Source, we are all in the same "army."

Problems develop in some relationships because many people do not relate to one another as fellow soldiers involved in the same struggles, looking toward the same victory. There are a lot of one-man armies in the marketplace today. Far too often when someone gets wounded in the battle, his "friends" are quick to finish him off with criticism, gossip, or judgment.

Soldiers share a special bond. They are together in dangerous and exhausting circumstances. Sometimes there are setbacks. Physical surroundings often leave much to be desired. But fellow soldiers do have some things going for them. They are focused on a common goal. They recognize a common enemy, and many are willing to unselfishly give their lives for a friend.

Author and lecturer Landon Saunders tells the story of two soldier friends, fighting side by side in a battle. When a hand grenade went off nearby, they ran for cover. One made it safely, but the other fell, gravely wounded. When the friend who made it realized his buddy hadn't, he started back to get him. An officer warned him not to go, but he went anyway.

Later he returned, carrying the lifeless body of his friend. He himself had received a mortal wound.

"You see, it wasn't worth it," the officer said. To which the dying man replied, "Oh, yes, it was worth it, because, you see, when I got to his side, his last words were, 'Jim, I knew you'd come.'"[4]

Our Most Important Relationship

Author Max Lucado tells about his boyhood days when he would wait for his dad to get home from work in the afternoons. His father would arrive and dole out snacks from his leftover lunch. He would put his straw hat on Max's head and his boots on the boy's feet. It was all a five-year-old boy could want. Then Max poses a question:

But suppose, for a minute, that is all I got. Suppose my dad, rather than coming home, just sent some things home. Boots for me to play in. A hat for me to wear. Snacks for me to eat. Would that be enough? Maybe so, but not for long. Soon the gifts would lose their charm. Soon, if not immediately, I'd ask, "Where's Dad?"

Imagine God making us a similar offer:

I will give you anything you desire. . . . You will never be afraid or alone. You will never lack for anything. . . . You will never be lonely. You will never die.

Only you will never see my face.

Would you want it? Neither would I. It's not enough. . . . What we want is God. . . . It's not that the perks aren't attractive. It's just that they aren't enough. It's not that we are greedy. It's just that we are his and—Augustine was right—our hearts are restless until they rest in him.[5]

Ultimately, life is all about relationships, and our most important one is with the One who created us. He loves us more than we can imagine, and He wants us to be in peaceful relationship with Himself, with ourselves, and with others.

If we will allow Him, He will bless us to this end.

A Pat
on the Back

*I thank my God, making mention of you always in my
prayers, hearing of your love and faith which you have
toward the Lord Jesus and toward all the saints, that
the sharing of your faith may become effective by the
acknowledgment of every good thing which is in you in
Christ Jesus. For we have great joy and consolation in
your love, because the hearts of the saints have been
refreshed by you, brother.*
—Philemon 4–7

CHAPTER FOUR

LEARN TO AFFIRM

*I*T WAS THE 1960s. What a time to be in high school! Those were the days of pep rallies and pom-poms, glass pack mufflers and drag races, Bass Weejuns and Levis, hayrides and the Beatles, and . . . high school English! Well, we couldn't have everything the way we wanted it.

When it was time to do my English homework, I would much rather have been, in the words of Petula Clark, "downtown, where all the lights are bright."

My high school English teacher's name was Miss Ava White. She had devoted her life to teaching high school English and had developed quite a reputation around my hometown for being a strict, no-nonsense disciplinarian.

During the first half of the year, I didn't apply myself in her class. I had a very active social life, I seldom studied, and in my immaturity, I sought to just "get by." I remember well the day Miss White told me to stay after class. I immediately thought, *I know what this means. She's going to give me a piece of her mind for my poor conduct and grades and probably accompany it with a pink slip and a trip to the vice principal's office.*

I knew what would happen there, having been the recipient of his discipline before. Those were the days when corporal punishment was common in public schools.

When everyone had left, Miss White called me to her desk, looked me square in the eyes, and said, "Son, you have character. You are smart. And I know you are capable of doing far better work than you are doing. I just want you to know that I believe in you and am confident you can be an A student if you would just try harder."

Wow! She believed in me. And that pat on the back after class did more for me than I could ever put into words. Miss White and I started meeting after school. Not wanting any of my friends to know, I would sneak up the back stairwell at the end of the day to her room on the third floor. Each day she spent an hour teaching me how to outline and think analytically.

She believed in me, and she let me know it. In no time my grades soared from C's to A's. To this very day every time I outline a book or write a chapter, I am indebted to Miss Ava White. She changed my life and the way I viewed myself with a few simple words of encouragement.

The Power of an Affirming Word

Affirmation is essential to positive relationships. Paul recognizes this, and his letter to Philemon begins with these supportive words: "I thank my God, making mention of you always in my prayers" (v. 4).

Paul's attitude of gratefulness is central to his fellowship with God and with others. Having a thankful spirit gets the focus off ourselves and onto God and what He has done for us. Thankfulness says something about people: that they recognize God as Lord and provider, and they are willing to humble themselves and acknowledge what He has done. It shows that they are spiritually alive.

Larry McKenzie, a minister in Memphis, Tennessee, has a unique answer to the daily question "How are you?" His response? "Grateful." And the light in his eyes shows that he means it.

King David penned more words of thanksgiving in Scripture than anyone else. Psalm 30:4 so typifies his attitude:

> *Sing praise to the LORD, you saints of His,*
> *And give thanks at the remembrance of His holy name.*

Cultivating an attitude of thanksgiving will draw us nearer to God's heart and eclipse negative attitudes and feelings more quickly than almost anything else.

Hearing of someone's thankfulness for you or for something you do gives a marvelous boost to the relationship. There's nothing you won't do for the person who is genuinely thankful for you.

Susan and Joanna had been in a Bible study with a few other women for some time. Although their relationship was cordial, there was not real closeness between them. One day, as the study was ending, Susan prayed, "I thank You for Joanna, and for her willingness to experience discomfort to reach out to others."

After that, the relationship was on a different plane. A new friendship and appreciation grew between them. Joanna even invited Susan's family to go camping with hers.

Paul was aware of the power of communion with God, and he knew the encouragement it would be to Philemon to know that he was regularly in Paul's prayers.

How do you feel when someone says she is praying for you? If you ask for prayers, you can hope that the person will do it. But what if a friend sees you and out of the blue says, "I always thank God as I remember you in my prayers"? You *know* that person is praying for you. What a lift it gives! And what a difference it makes in the relationship and in your feelings toward her!

Say It Like You Mean It

Paul was not vague in expressing admiration for his friend. The tense of the verb in the Greek tells Philemon that it was not just an arrow of thanks shot at random. Rather, it was pointed and sincere on Paul's part, and he didn't shrink back from letting his friend know it.

Appreciation is missing in many relationships, causing discouragement, misunderstandings, and strained friendships.

Ron is a case in point. As an accountant working for a friend in a small insurance company, he was used to the long hours, and he was not too surprised when the raise he was hoping for failed to materialize due to an economic slump. Ron quit after a year, though, with this explanation: "I didn't expect everything to be perfect, but it was hard to maintain my excitement and enthusiasm for the job because no one ever said *anything*, good or bad, about the job I was doing. Maybe I need more inward motivation, but I figured I could do just as well on my own."

Ron established his own accounting firm, and his friend lost a valuable worker because he failed to express appreciation for a job well done.

Start Off on the Right Foot

A lot of relational failures result from getting started on the "wrong foot." Some potential friendships crumbled at the outset through an awkward date, an ill-planned interview, or some other social clumsiness.

Even international negotiations often suffer from lack of mutual affirmation by the parties involved. That is certainly true, for example, in the struggle for a solution to the Israeli-Palestinian conflict, which has dominated world headlines for more than four decades. Here is one situation that, until recently, had been almost void of affirmation and understanding on either side, resulting in stagnation and standoff for years.

Mutual affirmation opened the door for the unprecedented peace accord signed in 1994. The Israeli leadership showed sympathy toward the Palestinians' plight. They recognized the Palestinians' right to individual dignity and some type of self-rule. And they acknowledged the tragedies of the massacres of villages like Deir Yassin where 250 women, children, and old men lost their lives in April 1948.

The Palestinian leadership recognized Israel's right to exist within safe and secure boundaries, genuinely retracting earlier statements about driving the Israelis into the sea. They acknowledged the modern Jewish struggle and the atrocities that took the lives of their fathers, mothers, brothers, and sisters in such places as Dachau and Treblinka. In short, they simply spoke some words of affirmation.

Perhaps this sounds a bit simplistic. But my point is, affirming someone else has an incredibly disarming effect and can become the launchpad for positive and fruitful relationships.

There is little hope for successful negotiation in any relationship that is characterized by heavy-handedness and a lack of charity. As premier of the Soviet Union in the late fifties and early sixties, Nikita Khrushchev did not get very far in his relationship with the United States with the comment, "We will bury you."

Paul makes certain that he does not start off on the wrong foot with Philemon. As the great apostle and as Philemon's father in the faith, Paul could have been tempted to pull rank on Philemon and give him orders. But his heart of love and concern for all involved wouldn't allow him to do that. He didn't even think of beginning the letter: "I know Onesimus cheated you, but as the apostle Paul, I'm telling you to take him back and get over it." No, he begins with warm, cordial words, putting Philemon at ease and pointing out his positive qualities.

Be Specific

Paul's words are not empty flattery. Philemon knew of Paul's sincerity because he was specific in his praise: "Hearing of your love and faith which you have toward the Lord Jesus and toward all the saints" (v. 5). Affirmation must be genuine to be effective.

Many secular volumes dealing with relationships within the marketplace are built on manipulation and are often dishonest in their approach to gain leverage over others. But these methods have no place in our relationships because we owe it to our fellow human beings to treat them with dignity and respect. Manipulative methods usually backfire anyway because most people can see through them. Make sure the pat on the back you give is unfeigned.

John, an engineer at a telecommunications company, had

read a book about winning others to his point of view through positive words. One morning in the hallway, he ran into Steve, who was a rung above him on the corporate ladder. "Steve, I think you're one of the most effective workers at the company," he blurted out. "Really?" was the reply. "In what way?" There was an awkward silence as John's mind raced for an answer. It became obvious that the compliment was an empty one.

Paul is careful not to make that kind of mistake with Philemon. He finds a character trait in Philemon that he can legitimately praise. He affirms Philemon's personal beliefs, and indirectly his life, by saying he is thankful for his faith in the Lord Jesus.

Be Loving

Genuine faith will prove itself with loving actions, and love is the glue that holds together all permanent relationships. People are able to truly love others because they are able to love themselves, and they can love themselves when it becomes obvious to them how much God loves them.

As a former idol-worshiping pagan, Philemon was keenly aware of the dramatic difference that God had made in his life through Christ. His gratitude and Spirit-filled life showed themselves in a gracious and kind nature that was obvious to everyone, and news of his good reputation had made it back to Paul. How pleased and how thankful Paul must have been to hear that his son in the faith was living such a godly life!

Parents do their best to train children to be responsible, faithful, and happy, but there comes a time to let them go, a moment of truth when the children are responsible for their actions. What a relief and joy it is to hear that they are doing well, that they are doing right.

Gayle, a widow in Houston, Texas, watched at the airport as her son Greg flew off to Germany one bright June morning. He was to work for a computer firm there for at least a year. Greg was twenty years old, and she wouldn't have made him stay in Houston with her even if she could have. But the apprehension on her face was unmistakable. What would his year away be like? Would the faith that she had instilled in him carry him through? Was Jesus a person to him or just a concept?

Four weeks later, Gayle held in her nervous hands a letter from the pastor of the church that Greg was attending. Tears filled her eyes as she read these words: "He's been such an asset to the church family here. . . . We already feel like he's one of us. You should feel very proud."

The book of Proverbs confirms, "As cold water to a weary soul,/ So is good news from a far country" (25:25). No doubt, Paul was delighted to hear secondhand of Philemon's faith and love.

Philemon's love for others was a result of his relationship with God. First John 4:7 tells us: "Beloved, let us love one another, for love is of God; and everyone who loves is born of God and knows God."

Love Without Prejudice

Paul mentions Philemon's love for "all" the saints. Philemon had good relationships because he didn't play favorites. He reached out in love not just to those who were popular and prosperous but to those who were powerless and poor.

James emphasizes the importance of this character trait:

*My brethren, do not hold the faith of our Lord Jesus
Christ, the Lord of glory, with partiality. . . . If you really
fulfill the royal law according to the Scripture, "You shall
love your neighbor as yourself," you do well; but if you
show partiality, you commit sin, and are convicted by the
law as transgressors. (James 2:1, 8–9)*

Paul commends Philemon's love for others before bringing up the touchy situation with Onesimus. Philemon's love
for "all the saints" will obviously include Onesimus, the
runaway former servant who is already on his way home in
remorse.

When it comes time for Philemon to meet the challenge of
accepting Onesimus, Paul's confident words about his character
will have long been etched onto his heart. What choice will
Philemon have but to receive Onesimus and restore the relationship?

All of us have friendships that have been tested in the fires
of estrangement from time to time. We've all been wronged
by a friend, relative, or ally in the faith. And we all know how
hard it is to show love and compassion for those who have hurt
us.

But the mark of true Christian character is the ability to
overcome differences with a brother or sister and move forward
in the relationship. When we learn to put aside our human
desires to shun or get even and instead shower our enemies with
love and mercy, we'll know that we are living in the will and
Spirit of God.

I encourage you today to do for someone else what Paul is
asking Philemon to do for Onesimus. Open your arms and your

heart to a brother in need of forgiveness. Shower a sister in the faith with love and kindness and compassion. Don't let another sun go down on your anger (see Eph. 4:26).

Show genuine love for "all" the saints in Christ. You will be surprised at the blessing it will bring to your life.

CHAPTER FIVE

REFRESHMENT
FOR THE HEART

*I*S IT POSSIBLE to be connected with the Creator of the universe through personal faith in His Son and not be active in sharing that faith?

The answer would seem to be an unequivocal no. And yet the word *evangelism* is a catalyst for much guilt and frustration among Christians today.

Paul addressed this issue with Philemon, too, by praying "that the sharing of your [Philemon's] faith may become effective." Another translation puts it this way: "I pray that you may be active in sharing your faith" (v. 6 NIV). The power of prayer for God's working in our hearts and lives is not to be underestimated or ignored.

Paul's encouragement of Philemon motivated him to be proactive in his relationships with others. Those who are in meaningful relationships share what is important to them, and Paul's assumption was that Philemon would begin to do just that.

Jesus reminded His followers that a truly wise person knew what he should do and became active in putting it into practice. Paul is challenging his friend Philemon to become the initiator in relationships. He knows that if Philemon is aware of "every good thing which is in you in Christ Jesus," that will catapult him toward a changed way of relating to others. As a result, their lives will be changed as well.

Your encouragement of others motivates them to try harder and do what they are capable of doing. That is why the most successful college football coaches over the long haul are leaders like Bobby Bowden of Florida State and Joe Paterno of Penn State, men who lead their young athletes by encouragement. Watch them on the sidelines as they move from player to player, patting them on the back and causing them to believe in themselves.

That is also why the most sought after public speakers are men like Zig Ziglar who inspire and affirm their hearers. That is the reason the most successful businessmen are men like Wayne Huizenga of Blockbuster Video and the Florida Marlins who motivate others to be better than they are. And that is why the best educators are people like Ava White who recognize the importance of giving a young teenager a pat on the back, even when he might not deserve it.

A Call to Action

Paul continues to challenge Philemon to be proactive in order to "have a full understanding of every good thing we have in Christ" (v. 6 NIV). He wants Philemon to know the joy and peace that come from being related to Christ. In Colossians 2:2–3, Paul tells Philemon and the other Christians in Colosse about his heart's desire:

> *That their hearts may be encouraged, being knit together in love, and attaining to all riches of the full assurance of*

*understanding, to the knowledge of the mystery of God,
both of the Father and of Christ, in whom are hidden all
the treasures of wisdom and knowledge.*

All the riches, complete understanding, knowledge of the mystery, and all the treasures—only an heir has access to these things. And these are what God wants us to share with the world.

When we share anything at all, from physical provisions to emotional needs, we make ourselves vulnerable to possible rejection, but we also act in faith that God's unlimited provision and mercy will meet our needs.

It is no different with our faith. We become partners in God's business of people, and we enter into a close relationship with Him of give-and-take that those who aren't on the line for Him cannot experience.

Much is under the surface of this statement in the opening paragraph of affirmation in Paul's letter to Philemon. Paul was anticipating asking Philemon to receive Onesimus later on in the letter. He was keenly aware that if Philemon possessed the "full assurance of understanding," he would have no recourse but to forgive and accept his runaway former servant. This phrase of the letter is filled with anticipation that Philemon will do the right thing.

A Call to Encouragement

As he continues to write, Paul warmly states, "For we have great joy and consolation in your love" (v. 7). Philemon has evidently shown great kindness and friendship to him, and Paul is not ashamed to talk about it.

We live in a macho world where it is not in vogue for men to express their love for one another. In many ways this is sad and even tragic because millions of men hunger for the friendship that could make all the difference in their lives.

Some time ago I drove my daughter, Holly, to a high school where her team was playing in a basketball tournament. As we drove into the parking lot I noticed a sign on the football stadium: "Brian Piccolo Field." Brian Piccolo was a Ft. Lauderdale, Florida, football hero a generation ago at St. Thomas High. He went on to an outstanding college career at Wake Forest University and then to the Chicago Bears of the National Football League. Alan McGinnis tells his story in his classic volume *The Friendship Factor*.

When Piccolo was on road trips with the Bears, his roommate was the great black Hall of Fame running back Gale Sayers. In those days of integration and racial strife, neither of them had ever had a close friend of another race. Their friendship developed into one of the best known in sports, and it is forever immortalized in the motion picture *Brian's Song*.

During the 1969 football season, Brian Piccolo was diagnosed with cancer. It was not unusual for Gale Sayers to fly to his bedside between games. They planned to sit together with their wives at the Professional Football Writers' annual dinner in New York City. There, Sayers was to receive the prestigious George Halas Award given to the most courageous player in professional football. But Brian did not make the dinner. He was confined to what would soon become his deathbed.

At the ceremony, Gale Sayers stood to receive his award and, with tears filling his eyes, said, "You flatter me by giving me this

52

award. But I tell you here and now that I accept it for Brian Piccolo. Brian Piccolo is the man of courage who should receive the George S. Halas Award. I love Brian Piccolo and I'd like you to love him. Tonight, when you hit your knees please ask God to love him too."[1]

Are there people in your circle of friends whose love has given you great joy and encouragement? Why not go ahead and tell them? Sit down, like Paul did, and write them a note of admiration. It will be there for them to read and reread. You might be surprised at the results.

A Call to Motivate

Recently, my wife, Susie, and I were guests of friends at Skibo Castle in the Scottish Highlands. It is the former home of the late, great Scottish-American industrialist Andrew Carnegie. I was particularly fascinated by the library, which contains much of Carnegie's personal correspondence. There I came across the name of Charles Schwab.

Charles Schwab worked for the multimillionaire Carnegie. He became the first man to earn a one-million-dollar salary—an astronomical amount at the turn of the century. One might be quick to assume that he knew more about the manufacturing of steel than anyone else in the world. Wrong! In fact, by his own admission there were many others with far greater technical know-how than his.

Why, then, would Andrew Carnegie pay Charles Schwab a million dollars a year? Schwab was paid such a handsome amount primarily because of his ability to motivate others into productive work habits and relationships.

Charles Schwab put his secret in his own words:

I consider my ability to arouse enthusiasm among men the greatest asset I possess. And the way to develop the best that is in a man is by appreciation and encouragement. There is nothing else that so kills the ambitions of men as criticism from their superiors. I never criticize anyone. I believe in giving a man incentive to work. So, I am anxious to find praise but loathe to find fault.[2]

Charles Schwab let others know what he liked about them and then positively motivated them to build the most successful industry in the entire world.

Many centuries before Schwab helped Carnegie build his financial dynasty by encouraging others, Paul used the same technique in this piece of correspondence to his friend Philemon. And it still works today.

Try building someone up the next time you are waiting for an office elevator or conversing with a waitress in your favorite restaurant. We touch the lives of people every day who have not heard a word of appreciation and admiration in years—and perhaps in a lifetime. Say it with a smile: "That is a beautiful dress." "You have such a pleasant voice."

Some of us go months and even years without giving a personal word of admiration to our spouses and then wonder why the relationship seems to be in a rut! Some parents allow their teenagers to graduate from high school and move away without any memory of affirmation from the people who matter most to them.

A simple compliment can make someone's whole day and boost the person's self-esteem. It can make your employees more productive in the office, your family more respectful and loving around the house, and your friends enjoy your company and look forward to being with you.

A Call to Refreshment

Paul continues his affirmation of Philemon by acknowledging that "the hearts of the saints have been refreshed by you, brother" (v. 7). He is letting his friend know that he enjoys his company and finds it, in his own words, "refreshing." He uses a Greek word here that carries with it the connotation of being relieved from pain.

Have you ever had a toothache, gone to the dentist, and had the problem solved? Talk about a refreshing feeling! Have you ever climbed a mountain and just before the summit thought you could not make it another step? But you did. Then you pulled out your bottle of water, gulped it down, and lay down in the grass with an exhilarating sense of accomplishment. All this is in the word Paul used to describe the effect Philemon had on him and others. Philemon refreshed the hearts of his friends.

I have known people who have been the embodiment of this phrase. Being in their very presence is a refreshing and beautiful experience.

My late friend, Gene Whiddon, had this effect on everyone who touched him. And when he died prematurely, literally thousands of people filed by his casket to pay their respects. They covered the gamut from United States senators to laborers, and they all had stories to tell about how this man had "refreshed" their lives.

How would you feel if you received a letter today that said, "We have great joy and consolation in your love, because the hearts of the saints have been refreshed by you"? How would that word of affirmation feel if it were directed at you?

Conversely, how would you feel if you received a letter that was unjustly caustic and critical? Which one would motivate you to be a better and more productive person?

One day while writing this book, I received a handful of letters in the mail. I opened the first one and found it to be extremely unjust. It wounded me greatly. I continued through the mail, and when I finished, I had read over a half dozen other letters that were filled with affirmation.

One letter writer indicated that she had gained the encouragement to try to mend the relationship with her estranged husband from a recent talk I had given. And she had done so! Others told of "miracles" that had taken place in their relationships when they put the principle of a pat on the back into practice. I can't tell you what those letters did for me. Words of affirmation have a powerful effect on the receiver.

Mark Twain, who left us volumes of quotes and quips, was never more on target than when he said, "I can live for two months on one good compliment!" As I sit at my computer thinking about the impact of encouraging words, my mind races back to an experience I haven't thought about in more than thirty years.

In my boyhood days in Fort Worth, Texas, I played Little League baseball. Our manager for the first two seasons was big and husky, rough and tough, and we were all afraid of him. He demanded the kind of perfection that a lot of ten year olds could not deliver. I was a very average ballplayer those first two years.

But my third and last year a new manager took over our team.

I remember well the team meeting Mr. Huffman called on the afternoon after our first game of the season. He called me to his side in front of all the other guys, patted me on the back, and said, "Did you see what Hawkins did last night? Instead of throwing home where we had little chance to get the runner out, he faked the throw and then threw to second, caught the base runner off guard, and got us out of the inning. Now, that is what I want us all to do. Think! Anticipate the play." And then with another pat on the back, he looked at me and said, "Great job!"

The coach believed in me! I can't tell you what that word of affirmation, that simple pat on the back, did for me. I played above my head that year and won the league batting title. It's not a big deal to anyone else, but it was a big deal for a twelve-year-old kid on the east side of Fort Worth. Never underestimate the power of positive affirmation in your relationships.

Christ As Our Example

The greatest encourager who ever lived was Jesus. That is why so many people flocked to Him. The religious phonies of His day felt uncomfortable around Him. But everyone else was refreshed in His presence. He spent his whole life telling others that God wanted their company and that they could make a new start.

One day in the village of Bethany a woman came to Him and anointed His feet with very expensive perfume that cost the equivalent of a year's salary in the first-century world. Several people began to rebuke her for what they considered to be a waste. How do you think that woman felt when Jesus looked into her eyes and said, "[You have] done a beautiful thing to me" (Matt. 26:10 NIV)? Talk about renewing a person's spirit! That is why she later followed Him all the way to the cross, even when most of His disciples had left.

And what about the woman caught in the act of adultery? The legalists of the day had their fingers pointed at her in accusation and were preparing to execute their judgment. How it must have affected her when Jesus interrupted the proceedings, got rid of them, then saw her repentant heart and said, "I don't condemn you. But go and sin no more" (John 8:11). Perhaps for the first time in her life, someone gave her a word of affirmation, and it changed her destiny. She, too, was one of the women faithful to the very end.

Then there was Simon Peter, the fisherman. He had been so self-confident. But when the chips were down, he caved in and denied he knew Jesus. How relieved he must have been when some days later Jesus met him on the shore and let Peter know that his failure wasn't fatal. Peter was never the same again, and he went from that encounter to become the undisputed leader of first-generation Christianity.

The Power of a Pat on the Back

It is no surprise that Paul begins his letter on interpersonal relationships with a significant note of affirmation. Something about our very makeup calls out for recognition.

Athletes need affirmation. When they know the coach believes in them, they amaze the crowds. Musicians need it. When the director believes in them, they move the audience with their music. Students thrive on affirmation. A teacher who believes in them can change their study habits and sometimes their lives. Employees crave it. When the boss appreciates them, they take pride in their work.

Children flourish in an atmosphere of kind, positive words. When they know that Mom and Dad believe in them, they want to obey. Husbands and wives need to be affirmed. When their spouses believe in them they love better. It is true in any kind of relationship on earth. A pat on the back has a supernatural motivating power about it.

Look around you. There are people in your world who have lived months and perhaps years without anyone, any-where, anytime, affirming them. They are looking for it and longing for it. Go ahead. Make someone's day! Try it this week.

Do you know someone with a broken heart or a broken dream or even a broken life? Someone in crisis? Someone who is desperate? Someone who is hanging by a thread with hope almost gone? If you do not offer affirmation in some way right now, perhaps no one else in their world ever will.

You may be thinking, *I wish someone would pat me on the back like that.* But when you find someone to affirm, you might be surprised at how quickly the action will be reciprocated and you'll begin to reap what you sow.

The problem with many of us in our interpersonal relation-ships is that we are reactive and not proactive. We sit around waiting for others to take the initiative so that we can react to them. And guess what? They are waiting for us!

Author Jim Woodruff once said that a mentally healthy person looks for someone to love, and a mentally unhealthy person looks for someone to love him or her.

Take a tip from Paul. Encourage others to be the best they

can be, to do the best they can do, to live the best lives they can live. Give someone a word of appreciation and encouragement. Sit down and write a thank-you note or make a phone call to lighten the load of a friend. The results may change someone's life.

Including yours!

Win-Win Relationships

*Therefore, though I might be very bold in Christ to com-
mand you what is fitting, yet for love's sake I rather appeal to you—being such a one as Paul, the aged, and
now also a prisoner of Jesus Christ—I appeal to you for
my son Onesimus, whom I have begotten while in my
chains, who once was unprofitable to you, but now is
profitable to you and to me.*
—Philemon 8–11

CHAPTER SIX

THE GAMES
PEOPLE PLAY

*H*OW MANY OF US truly understand the impact of our words and actions on those around us? Do we really grasp the importance of treating others with love and respect in a relationship? Do we comprehend the power of a simple word of affirmation or a well-placed pat on the back? And do we know the consequences of never relaying those kinds of positive, life-affirming acts of kindness to others?

Every now and then a story comes along that confirms once again for me the crucial need for positive interpersonal skills in our society—as parents, spouses, leaders, businesspersons, and Christians. And few stories relay that need more vividly than one told by Helice Bridges.

It began with a teacher in New York who decided to honor each of the seniors in her high school. She called them one by one to the front of the class and affirmed them for their unique contributions to the school. Then she presented each of them with a blue ribbon imprinted with gold letters that read, "Who I Am Makes A Difference."

Afterward she gave each student three more ribbons and

encouraged the seniors to go out and spread this ceremony of acknowledgment. They were to find one person who touched their lives and present a ribbon. Then they were to give that person some extra ribbons, encouraging the person to do the same.

The process began, and somewhere down the line a junior executive for a large firm found himself with some ribbons. He decided to acknowledge his boss, a man known for his gruff and grouchy demeanor. He sat his boss down and told him how much he admired his creative genius. He then thanked him for the impact he'd made on his life and pinned the ribbon on to his superior's coat, right above his heart.

The boss was moved by this act, and he quickly agreed to take an extra ribbon to pass on to someone else.

That night, on his way home from work, he decided to honor his fourteen-year-old son. The boy had seemed depressed lately, and the man knew he wasn't giving his son enough affirmation and love. This would be a good opportunity to relay his feelings for the boy, he thought.

Later that evening, he sat his son down in the living room and told him,

The most incredible thing happened to me today. I was in my office and one of the junior executives came in and told me he admired me and gave me a blue ribbon for being a creative genius. Then he put this blue ribbon that says "Who I Am Makes A Difference" on my jacket. He gave me an extra ribbon and asked me to find somebody else to honor. As I was driving home tonight, I started thinking about whom I would honor with this ribbon and I thought about you. I want to honor you.

My days are really hectic and when I come home I don't pay a lot of attention to you. Sometimes I scream at you for not getting good enough grades in school and for your bedroom being a mess, but somehow tonight, I just wanted to sit here and, well, just let you know that you do make a difference to me. Besides your mother, you are the most important person in my life. You're a great kid and I love you!

The startled boy began to sob and sob, and he couldn't stop crying. His whole body shook. He looked up at his father and said through his tears, "I was planning on committing suicide tomorrow, Dad, because I didn't think you loved me. Now I don't need to."[1]

I'll bet that father didn't soon forget his boy's need for affirmation. He probably began spending less time at the office and more time patting his son on the back. And that conversation no doubt still serves as a haunting reminder to him of the need to verbalize his love and commitment to others (especially his family) instead of assuming that they know.

It should do the same for us. We should never forget the importance of relating positively with others—of confirming our love and respect for them as we communicate on a daily basis.

Playing to Win

Paul's letter to Philemon is rich in advice on the practical how-tos of developing and maintaining positive relationships with others. So far we've examined the importance of getting off to a good start through affirmation. And we've seen the disarming effect a pat on the back can have. Now, this master motivator of men builds on this foundation by showing the importance of what can be called the win-win philosophy of relationships.

His letter to Philemon continues, "Therefore, though I might be very bold in Christ to command you what is fitting, yet for love's sake I rather appeal to you . . . I appeal to you for my son Onesimus, . . . who once was unprofitable to you, but now is profitable to you and to me" (vv. 8–11).

Paul appeals to his friend on the basis of an ongoing relationship in which there will be no losers. Everyone can be successful. Everyone can prosper. Playing win-win with others in the game of life is the only way to play.

Paul knows this fact, and he is intent on helping Philemon understand his genuine desire for peace in this strained relationship. He wants Philemon to know that life doesn't have to be filled with anger and resentment toward others. Forgiving others of their faults is essential for healthy relationships. Nobody wins when we hold grudges. Everybody wins when we love and forgive.

The problem with most strained relationships is that people forget this fact. We forget that relating positively with others means keeping everyone's interest in mind—playing win-win in all of our dealings with others. One-sided relationships don't work. Mutually beneficial ones do.

Let's take a closer look at some of the many different ways of relating, many of which are unprofitable and damaging to everyone.

Competition: A Win-Lose Proposition

Some relationships are built on competition. This type of

relationship has been popularly called a win-lose relationship. That is, some will stay in a relationship only where they always win and the other person loses.

Bully Bob plays on this particular turf. As long as he is always on top, always on center stage, and always in control, he will continue in a relationship. But let the other party win just once, and the relationship is in serious trouble.

Bully Bob has to win every argument and always be right. In fact, it is not enough that he always wins; he is not fully content unless the other side loses. Have you ever tried to relate to someone like Bully Bob who always has to win at someone else's expense?

Queen Jezebel of Israel tried to play this way. Her husband, Ahab, wanted a vineyard that was neither ethical nor legal for him to own. When Naboth, the owner, refused to sell, Jezebel lied and murdered to get it for Ahab.

Naboth lost. He paid for the defense of his family's inheritance with his life. But Jezebel and Ahab lost, also. For their unconscionable actions, God promised and delivered their violent deaths.

Why won't relationships based on such heavy-handedness work in the long run? Everyone involved eventually ends up losing.

Take, for example, a husband and a wife in a competitive win-lose relationship. He constantly orders her around the house. He coerces and controls. After a while, resentment begins to simmer and inevitably reaches a boiling point.

All these years he thinks he has won. But he wakes up one day to find that she has finally had enough, and she leaves, never to return. In the end, they both end up losing.

Bully Bob's relationship with his son is characterized by the same bullheadedness. Since Bob knows only how to play win-lose, he keeps his thumb on the youngster. He manipulates, controls, and gives orders. Resentment builds in the boy with every passing year of adolescence. As soon as the son is old enough to leave home, he hits the door, never to return. Tragically, he may spend a lifetime estranged from his dad.

Bully Bobs throw their weight around in the business world as well. They enjoy the thought of making others jump at their commands, and they don't feel successful unless others fear them. Although these people are feared, they are also resented and sometimes hated. They rarely motivate the productivity that would be possible with a different attitude.

One prominent American CEO had this to say about what it takes to keep others motivated and on track:

> If you want to get someone's attention, threats and intimidation will certainly do that. But if you want to build a lasting work relationship, based on mutual trust and respect, you'll do irreparable damage. You'll get results, but they'll be temporary and short-range.
>
> In our company, for example, let's assume a salesman is not making any sales. I can call him in and "dress him down." I can say, "Look, if you don't double your sales in the next month, I'll fire you." Because I'm in charge, and because he may need the job, he might go out and work extra hard to double his sales.
>
> But I've totally destroyed my relationship with that guy because he never knows when I'm going to pull something

like that again. He doesn't have any security. And I've built a barrier of fear and resentment between us that I may never be able to cross again.

But if I took that same guy and spent that time talking about the fantastic opportunities available to him and explaining what a bright future he has if he can just get his sales up, he'll wind up going out and making three times as many sales as he would have with fear as a motivator. Plus, I've built a positive relationship in which he can continue to grow and develop.[2]

In a win-lose relationship, everyone eventually loses.

Compromise: A Lose-Win Proposition

Some relationships are built on compromise. This type of connection could be referred to as a lose-win relationship. Loser Larry tries to relate to others on this playing field. He is the fellow with the martyr complex. His self-esteem is so damaged that he feels the only way he can maintain a relationship with someone is to always put himself down and let the other person win.

Have you ever known anyone like Loser Larry? He is to be pitied. He is always walking around on eggshells, insincerely patting the other party on the back, constantly lifting the other person up in the hope that, in turn, he will be accepted. He earns scorn instead. He is a compromiser.

Dr. David Seamands writes about such a person:

Ben was one of the most timid souls I have ever counseled. I couldn't even hear him. "What did you say, Ben?". . . He was so afraid to be a burden to people. It could make a person uncomfortable to be around him. You might look to see if he was wearing a sandwich board that read, "Excuse me for living."

Have you ever heard of the "Dependent Order of Really Meek and Timid Souls"? When you make an acrostic of its first letters, you have "Doormats." The Doormats have an official insignia—a yellow caution light. Their official motto is: "The meek shall inherit the earth, if that's OK with everybody!" . . .

Well, Ben could have been a charter member of the Doormats.[3]

Why won't relationships built on compromise produce lasting results? In the end, everyone involved ends up losing. Loser Larry gives the store away until there is nothing left. And in the process, his "friends" lose all respect for him.

The woman from Sychar who talked at the well with Jesus was a victim of her own compromise. She possessed such low self-esteem that she continued in the loser's bracket while allowing the men of the town to use her.

Life changed for her, though, during a conversation with the Inventor of winning relationships. She ran back to the very people with whom she had played her games of compromise and introduced them to the One who had changed her life. Many people in the town put their faith in Christ because of her willingness to talk about what He had done for her.

Complacency: A Lose-Lose Proposition

Other relationships are built on complacency. These are

sometimes referred to as lose-lose relationships. Miserable Marvin can be found on this court. He is the guy who is more interested in seeing you lose than in seeing himself win. Misery loves company. He never puts anything into a relationship and never expects anything out of one.

Miserable Marvin is basically a loser like Larry. However, what makes him different is that he will relate to you only as long as you are a loser too. As soon as some good fortune comes your way, he will cut you off at the pass. He has lost in life, and his low level of self-confidence enables him to find a comfort level only with other losers. He spends his life this way.

Don Aslett, businessman, author, and philosopher, talks about the Miserable Marvins of the world in one of his popular books:

> Living to be productive and happy is a struggle—full of tests, obstacles, and sacrifices. Those who have chosen junk standards, who have chosen not to be industrious, constructive, or honest, have chosen a loser's path to travel. They're not necessarily bad people, but they're keeping their lives like most of us keep our belongings—a lot of junk mixed in. This makes interaction with them uninspiring, if not unbearable.[4]

Why won't relationships based on complacency work in the long run? You guessed it! Everyone eventually ends up losing. Life loses its spirit of conquest and challenge. Complacency sets in and iron no longer sharpens iron (see Prov. 27:17). Relationships built on complacency never produce any real winners.

Capitulation: A Quitter's Game

Still other relationships are built on capitulation. Flake-Out Fred plays on this field. He is a quitter. If things get too hard or don't go his way, he goes home. He capitulates. Have you seen him around? He has been involved in a hundred different relationships and deals. Every new one is the one he has been waiting for. He plunges in with uncontrolled enthusiasm for a few days or weeks. Then he quits and starts looking for the next one.

This person is unstable and undisciplined. It's easier for him to just walk away and quit than to hang in there and make it work. Relationships based on capitulation never produce lasting results.

The prophet Elijah was tempted to give up one day. He had gotten off to a great start, bringing a dead boy back to life and winning a contest with the priests of Baal on Mount Carmel in an awesome and terrifying display of God's power.

But soon there came a threat from the murderous queen Jezebel, and Elijah tried to drop out of the game. He isolated himself from everyone he knew, sat under a tree alone, and asked God to take his life. When he got to the end of his rope, it happened: he met the Lord and went from there to the greatest mountaintop experiences of his career (see 1 Kings 18–19).

I like the story Bill Anderton tells about what really causes a person to give up and quit:

> It seems that one day the devil decided to go out of business, and he decided to sell all his tools to whomever would pay the price. On the night of the sale, they were all attractively displayed. Malice, hate, envy, jealousy, greed, sensuality,

and deceit were among them. To the side lay a harmless wedge-shaped tool, which had been used much more than any of the rest.

Someone asked the devil, "What's that? It's priced so high."

The devil answered, "That's discouragement."

"But why is it priced so much higher than the rest?" the onlooker persisted.

"Because," replied the devil, "with that tool I can pry open and get inside a person's consciousness when I couldn't get near with any of the others. Once discouragement gets inside, I can let all the other tools do their work."[5]

Second Chronicles 20 tells a fascinating story of standing strong in the face of discouragement. King Jehoshaphat is told, "A great multitude is coming against you from beyond the sea, from Syria; and they are in Hazazon Tamar" (v. 2).

Jehoshaphat was concerned by the message because he knew his army was no match for those enemies. Dismay and discouragement fell across the land, and Jehoshaphat knew he needed to do something, so he called for a fast among the people of Judah.

When they came together to seek help from the Lord, he stood up in front of them acknowledging the sovereignty and power of God. At the conclusion of his speech, Jehoshaphat said, "For we have no power against this great multitude that is coming against us; nor do we know what to do, but our eyes are upon You" (v. 12).

After that, the Spirit of the Lord came upon Jahaziel, son of Zechariah, who reported God's message:

> *Thus says the LORD to you: "Do not be afraid nor dismayed because of this great multitude, for the battle is not yours, but God's. Tomorrow go down against them. They will surely come up by the Ascent of Ziz, and you will find them at the end of the brook before the Wilderness of Jeruel. You will not need to fight in this battle. Position yourselves, stand still and see the salvation of the LORD, who is with you, O Judah and Jerusalem!" Do not fear or be dismayed; tomorrow go out against them, for the LORD is with you. (vv. 15–17)*

God delivered on that promise. As they stood on the battlefield the next morning singing praises to God, the Lord set ambushes against the army coming against them. Before long their enemies were defeated, and Jehoshaphat's army went home unscathed.

All of us feel discouraged from time to time and feel like quitting. Capitulation often seems like the easiest course of action in a desperate situation. But during those times, we need to take a cue from Jehoshaphat and look to God for the strength we need.

Don't be a Flake-Out Fred. Quitting is never the answer.

Cooperation: Everybody Wins

Is there a better way of forging and conducting relationships? Indeed there is! Life's most positive and productive relationships are built on cooperation. This is what we call a win-win relationship. Wise William knows how to play this game.

Paul was the captain of this team in the first century, and the game plan is woven throughout the fabric of the letter to

Philemon. Paul said to Philemon about Onesimus: "[He] once was unprofitable to you, but now is *profitable to you and to me*" (v. 11, emphasis mine). Such relationships are mutually beneficial. Wise William knows that when the other party wins in a relationship he ends up winning too.

Have you ever known anyone like Wise William? He is the man who wins by helping others win. As a husband, Wise William is not in competition with his wife. He seeks the best for her because he is smart enough to realize that when she wins and is happy, he ends up a winner too.

As a dad, he respects the individuality of his son. He doesn't try to force the boy to make up for what he hasn't accomplished. He is secure enough to pass on a positive self-image to his offspring, and he will share in the victories. He'll be a winner as a dad.

At the office, William is the businessman who wants his customers to win so he can stay in business. He sets his prices fairly and tries to give his customers good service. He knows that he needs them as much as they need him. In every deal he wants everyone to come out a winner.

Cooperation works! It is the only realistic approach to mutually beneficial friendships. All the players end up on the winning team. There are no losers. Cooperation is the key to victory and success, whether you are a family member at the kitchen table, a socialite at the bridge table, an executive at the conference table, or a diplomat at the peace table.

Winning with Christ

It doesn't matter how you have played the game thus far. You can get on the winning team today. It is never too late for a new beginning! Jesus of Nazareth is not some musty character from bygone days who is irrelevant to our lives in a twenty-first-century world. He is alive and can do for us today what He did for so many people so long ago.

Each time He met people He placed them in a winning relationship. He went around lifting people up from their boredom, discouragement, and failure, causing them to relate healthily and productively to others.

Paul got on the same team, and in his personal letter to Philemon, he passed the ball on to him. He reveals several important principles of winning relationships in his letter to Philemon. And in the next chapter we will examine them, focusing on how they can help us change our relationships for the better as well.

CHAPTER SEVEN

THE ONLY WAY TO WIN

*T*ERRY DOBSON was a student of Aikido, a Japanese art of self-defense. Aikido, he had been taught, is the practice of reconciliation, not retaliation. You don't try to dominate people with it; you defuse them. You resolve conflicts instead of starting them.

Though Terry excelled in practice, he never had to use the art outside classes. He had always wondered what would happen in a real confrontation. He was confident of his skill, but it looked as if he would never have a chance to test it—until, that is, a spring day on a Tokyo train.

At one station the doors opened and into the car burst a large man who was so inebriated that he was staggering. He was screaming at the top of his lungs, and he began swinging at some seated passengers. He came inches from landing a violent kick into the back of an elderly woman.

Without hesitation, Terry stood and faced the man. His years of training had convinced him that he could bring the drunk down within minutes. In his heart, he was even looking forward to finally getting to use his talents at Aikido.

But suddenly, before he had a chance to make the first move, a small old Japanese man called out to the drunk. "Hey!" he yelled, as though seeing an old friend. "C'mere and talk with me!"

The large drunk planted his feet belligerently in front of the old man and roared, "Why should I talk to you?"

The little man smiled widely at the drunk. "What'cha been drinking?" he asked, his eyes sparkling with interest.

"I been drinking sake," the drunk bellowed, "and it's none of your business!"

"Oh, that's wonderful," the old man persisted, still smiling. "I love sake too. Every night me and my wife warm up a little bottle of sake and take it out into the garden, and we sit on an old wooden bench. We watch the sun go down, and we look to see how our persimmon tree is doing. My great-grandfather planted that tree, and we worry about whether it will recover from those ice storms we had last winter. Our tree has done better than I expected, though. Especially when you consider the poor quality of the soil. . . ."

For several minutes the old man talked kindly to the drunk. Soon the man's face began to soften and his fists slowly unclenched. "I love persimmons too . . . ," he said, his voice trailing off as he spoke.

Terry watched in amazement as the old, gentle man disarmed a volatile situation with his kind and sincere words. Before long, the drunk was crying in the man's arms, telling him of his despair—the death of his wife, the loss of his job, the shame he felt when he drank.

The last Terry saw of the two, the drunk was sprawled out on the seat with his head in the old man's lap. The old man was softly stroking his filthy matted hair.

"As the train pulled away," Terry writes, "I sat down on a bench in the station. What I had wanted to do with muscle had been accomplished with kind words. I had just seen Aikido in action, and the essence of it was love."[1]

What a beautiful illustration of how to effectively and lovingly deal with people! We could all gain a barrelful of wisdom from that old Japanese man about relating to others with love and compassion and kindness. And if we took his advice to heart, all of our relationships would be better and stronger. Like the old man, we'd understand the power and beauty of relationships built on win-win principles.

A Sensitive Appeal

Paul is showing that same restraint and insight in his words to Philemon. "Therefore," he writes, "though I might be very bold in Christ to command you what is fitting, yet for love's sake I rather appeal to you" (vv. 8–9).

Paul knew that he could have pulled rank on Philemon, exerting his apostolic authority. It would have been the easy thing to do. It would have been the efficient thing to do. But he wanted to be sensitive and respect Philemon's rights as a person and a Christian. Paul wanted Philemon to do the right thing, but he wanted it to be his decision. So he didn't command; he encouraged.

In essence, Paul tells his friend, "I could be bold and order you to do what you ought to do. But I refuse to do it. I want everyone in this situation to emerge a winner." Paul was sensitive to the fact that people cannot be bullied or coerced if the relationship is to be a positive one.

Sensitivity is essential to all successful relationships. But many people have a drill sergeant approach to relationships. They like to give orders and watch others squirm and jump. Some actually take pride in this method and think they are winning along the way. Like Bully Bob from the previous chapter, they get their way through intimidation and coercion. They are the drunks on the Tokyo trains of life.

But Paul knew better. Had Philemon been compelled, with no say of his own in the matter, what kind of relationship do you think would have developed? It would have been built on coercion and guilt; ultimately, it would have had a damaging effect on all the relationships involved.

Making Things Right

With his careful choice of words, Paul appealed to Philemon in several positive ways. One was "for love's sake." Philemon's name meant "the loving one." Paul was asking him to live up to his name and to show the same loving attitude toward Onesimus that he had shown in the past to others.

Paul is not requesting that Onesimus be absolved of his previous wrongs without remorse or restitution. He will shortly offer to pay Onesimus's debt, but right now, he is encouraging Philemon to respond out of a commitment to treating others in a Christlike way and to do what he knows he should do.

How many of our own interpersonal problems would be solved if each of us would simply do what we ought to do? Most of us know how we should treat others, but we get stuck on the application of that knowledge. We know what it takes to make and keep friends, but we sometimes have trouble actually doing it.

Our kids need a great deal of our time and energy to grow

into healthy, productive people. Yet it's often all we can do to tear ourselves away from the office to be with them.

We know that our spouses need love and affirmation from us, but we don't always do well at giving it. We know that we need to patch strained and broken relationships, but often we can't seem to find the time and motivation to do so. And we don't necessarily want to be the first to open those lines of communication.

Knowing what we ought to do and doing it are two different matters. It's the latter hurdle we need to work on the most.

Paul knows how hard it is to do the right thing. And so he takes it upon himself to appeal to his brothers in Christ for reconciliation.

He encourages Onesimus to do what is necessary to make things right—that is, to face up to his mistakes and go back to Philemon in genuine remorse asking for forgiveness even though it won't be easy.

And he encourages Philemon to do the right thing. He asks him to receive the repentant Onesimus, in Paul's words, "no longer as a slave but more than a slave, as a beloved brother" (v. 16).

That is no small task for either of them. But it is important for them to address if the Spirit of love and unity is to reign among the fellowship of believers.

Giving Up Our "Rights"

Many of us have lived our lives with few lasting relationships because of our desire to control others. The lack of sensitivity is rampant in all types of relationships today. Insisting on one's own "rights" is the order of the day. When we realize that we have given our rights over to the Master of our lives, we will be freed to be the sensitive people that He wants us to be.

Philemon must put aside pride and a substantial economic advantage for the sake of harmony and fellowship with a Christian brother. Are we willing to deny ourselves any rights for the same reason?

Paul used another interesting choice of words when he wrote, "Yet for love's sake I rather *appeal* to you" (v. 9, emphasis mine). The Greek word he used for "appeal" is a rather strong one. It appears 108 times in the New Testament, and it is translated as "plead" or "strongly urge" or "encourage."

In our own efforts to win friends and influence people, the way in which we make our appeal is of utmost importance. Some people waste valuable time attempting to appeal to others strictly on the basis of reason. Others state their cases on the basis of merit, who they are or where they are from. Still others do so on the basis of tenure.

How do you go about winning people to your point of view? Do you appeal in love? Do you encourage based on reason or logic? Do you simply pull rank and tell them what to do? Take a cue from Paul. Learn the value of a well-thought-out phrase presented with sensitivity and love.

Overcoming Through Love

Paul also teaches us to appeal to others on the basis of love. The Greeks have several words that can be translated into English as "love." Paul chose the word that represents the highest level of love. It is best defined as "no matter what others may do to you by insult or injury, you seek for them only their highest good." This love is submissive and seeks the other's best.

Chuck Swindoll tells the story of a time when he, Dr. Bruce Waltke, who is a Hebrew scholar, and two other evangelical ministers arrived for a tour of the mother church of the First Church of Christ Scientist in downtown Boston. The elderly woman who conducted the tour had no idea who the men were or what their professions were. Swindoll described what took place:

She showed us several interesting things on the main floor. When we got to the multiple-manual pipe organ, she began to talk about their doctrine and especially their belief about no judgment in the life beyond. Dr. Waltke waited for just the right moment and very casually asked:

"But, Ma'am, doesn't it say somewhere in the Bible, 'It is appointed unto man once to die and after that, the judgment?'" He could have quoted Hebrews 9:27 in Greek! But he was so gracious, so tactful with the little lady. I must confess, I stood back thinking, "Go for it, Bruce. Now we've got her where we want her!"

The lady, without a pause, said simply, "Would you like to see the second floor?"

You know what Dr. Waltke said? "We surely would, thank you."

She smiled, somewhat relieved, and started to lead us up a flight of stairs.

I couldn't believe it! All I could think was, "No, don't let her get away. Make her answer your question!" As I was wrestling within, I pulled on the scholar's arm and said in a low voice, "Hey, why didn't you nail the lady? Why didn't you press the point and not let her get away until she answered?"

Quietly and calmly he put his hand on my shoulder and whispered, "But, Chuck, that wouldn't have been fair. That wouldn't have been very loving, either—now would it?"

Wham! The quiet rebuke left me reeling. I shall *never* forget that moment. And . . . in less than twenty minutes he was sitting with the woman alone, tenderly and carefully speaking with her about the Lord Jesus Christ. She sat in rapt attention. He, the gracious peacemaker, had won a hearing. And I, the scalp-snatcher, had learned an unforgettable lesson.

Do you know what she saw in my friend? A living representation of one of God's sons . . . exactly as God promised in his beatitude . . . "*they shall be called sons of God.*"[2]

This type of love epitomized Jesus' actions. He could play win-lose with us. He could order us to obey Him. He could pull our strings like a puppeteer to force us to shape up and get in step.

But what does He do instead? He shows us with His own life how to be submissive for another's good. He appeals to us on the basis of love. He gives us an invitation: "Come to Me, all you who labor and are heavy laden, and I will give you rest. Take My yoke upon you and learn from Me, for I am gentle and lowly in heart, and you will find rest for your souls" (Matt. 11:28–29). This type of love breaks down barriers and cements relationships.

James 3:17 says, "But the wisdom that is from above is first pure, then peaceable, gentle, *willing to yield*, full of mercy and good fruits, without partiality and without hypocrisy" (emphasis mine). Paul had this wisdom, and it showed itself in the way that the broken relationships were reconciled.

Love has its own way of finding out what is right and doing it. It is not a passive word; it is always equated with action. Love is something we do! When we submit to love, we do what we ought to do much more quickly and completely than when we are forced against our will to do something.

Paul continues playing on the field of winning relationships by saying, "I appeal to you for my son Onesimus, whom I have begotten while in my chains" (v. 10). Win-win friendships bring a bonding, a sense of family, and mutual support. By defending our friends, we bond ourselves with them.

Paul's description of Onesimus shows his unqualified support for him. He calls him "my own son." He carefully chooses a Greek word here that is a term of endearment. It means a small child. Thus, Paul is indicating to Philemon that Onesimus, who is on his way home, is still very young in the faith and needs support and love.

No Small Request

Paul is now coming to the purpose of his letter, and he is already nearly half through with it. This is the first mention of Onesimus.

Can you picture the wealthy aristocrat Philemon as he reads this letter for the first time? He is reading along and liking what he reads. This is good news! There is affirmation in every sentence. He is smiling and feeling very good about himself.

And then a name appears in the middle of the paragraph and leaps off the letter toward him.

Onesimus! That scoundrel! he thinks.

And it's not hard to understand his surprise. How would you feel if someone in whom you had placed your trust embezzled your money, left town, and was never heard from again? Then one day, out of the blue, you hear from another good friend and mentor, and the fugitive's name comes up.

Onesimus! That was the name Philemon could have gone years without hearing again.

But wait a minute. Paul says, "*My son* Onesimus." What is this? Philemon reads on, "Whom I have begotten while in my chains" Philemon must have said to himself, "I cannot believe it. It cannot be!"

Do you see what is happening? A broken relationship is about to be mended, and the catalyst, Paul, is supportive to both parties involved. He has shown his support for Philemon earlier by saying, "For we have great joy and consolation in your love, because the hearts of the saints have been refreshed by you, brother" (v. 7).

Now, he does the same thing for Onesimus by adding, "I appeal to you for my son Onesimus, whom I have begotten while in my chains, who once was unprofitable to you, but now is profitable to you and to me" (vv. 10–11).

Paul had shared with Onesimus in prison and was with him when he found a new life and a new beginning, when he was "born again." He was like a spiritual father to Onesimus, and therefore, he would stand for Onesimus like he would his own son.

Paul refers to Onesimus's previous service as "unprofitable."

Another translation of this word is "useless": "Formerly he was useless to you, but now he has become useful both to you and to me" (v. 11 NIV).

The Greek word Paul used to describe Onesimus as unprofitable or useless is the same word from which we derive our English word *archaic*. It portrays something or someone who has lost his usefulness and is therefore unserviceable.

But now, the old Onesimus is dead and buried. The swindling traitor that Philemon knew is long gone. In effect, Onesimus has become "serviceable" and "new." He is no longer outdated and "archaic." He has had new life breathed into him—the same new life that was breathed into Paul and Philemon. And in his body was a new creature in Christ, useful to everyone involved.

Paul wants Philemon to look at his former servant with a fresh eye and an open heart as if he were meeting him for the first time.

When anyone gets connected with God, coming into a vital relationship with Jesus Christ as Onesimus did, it does not produce a nebulous, inefficient, ineffective, useless person. It produces people who are "useful" to those around them.

Everybody Wins!

Does Paul win? Yes! He has the joy of mending the relationship between two men whom he has personally led to faith at different times and in different places. Had he resorted to giving orders instead of appealing in love, it would never have happened. Now he savors the love and support of both of them. He wins!

Does Philemon win? Yes! He gets Onesimus back, and this time Onesimus is profitable and useful to him. And he gets him back with repentance and restitution as well.

Does Onesimus win? Yes! He gets to come home. And what is more he returns, in Paul's words, "no longer as a slave but . . . a beloved brother" (v. 16).

There are no losers. These relationships are a model for successful reconciliations. They happen when we are sensitive and loving in our dealings with one another. They happen when we carefully choose our words in making a difficult request of a friend and when we treat people the way Christ would treat them.

Some have the idea that to put on the uniform of the Christian life is to play on the field of a lose-lose proposition. Ted Turner, television magnate and baseball owner, made headlines with his comment that "Christianity is for losers."

He is not the only one who shares this belief. People who go through life playing win-lose with others think Christianity is about religion—an archaic and lifeless religion at that.

And in many places and in many ways that is sadly true. "Religion" has often been a win-lose game. It has coerced, controlled, oppressed, obsessed, and virtually enslaved people through the centuries. It has been at the root of many world conflicts, and it continues today to be the cause of much confusion in places such as the Middle East.

Paul is not talking about "religion" in his letter to Philemon. He is interested in "relationships," and there is a world of difference.

Many people misunderstand Jesus for the same reason. He

was not about religion. In fact, He openly rebuked its excesses and perversions. He was, and still is today, about relationships.

How does this eternal connection with Jesus Christ work on a practical level? He plays win-win in His personal relationships with us. Like Paul, He is sensitive and loving. He doesn't order us into a relationship with Him. He appeals on the basis of love.

He submitted Himself to an earthly body, an earthly life, and a vicious execution in order to demonstrate His love and give us a future with hope.

And as Paul did for Onesimus, Jesus will stand by our side and call us family. He will never leave us or forsake us, and if we will come into a relationship with Him, He will one day stand in support of us before His Father's throne of judgment.

It just makes sense to put our faith and trust in Him. When we do, we will come to know how valuable we are and will be able to love others as well.

Burying
the Hatchet

*I am sending him back. You therefore receive him, that
is, my own heart, whom I wished to keep with me, that
on your behalf he might minister to me in my chains for
the gospel. But without your consent I wanted to do
nothing, that your good deed might not be by compulsion, as it were, but voluntary. For perhaps he departed
for a while for this purpose, that you might receive him
forever, no longer as a slave but more than a slave—a
beloved brother, especially to me but how much more to
you, both in the flesh and in the Lord.*

—Philemon 12–16

CHAPTER EIGHT

LOOKING FOR A FRESH START

"*L*ET'S JUST BURY the hatchet!" How many times have we heard that well-worn phrase? It carries with it the connotation of forgetting old scores and letting bygones be bygones.

The phrase finds its origin with Native Americans in the nineteenth century. When making peace, they would ceremoniously bury a hatchet in the earth to show that hostilities were over.

From this act of burying the hatchet comes our custom of shaking right hands when making peace, striking a deal, or settling a dispute. The right hand, the hatchet hand, is used to symbolically prove no weapon is being carried.

Thus, the phrase "bury the hatchet" has made its way into our Western colloquialism as a symbol of the mending of broken relationships.

Any relationship that is lasting and worthwhile over the years will have its moments of stress and brokenness. This is true in the relationship between a husband and a wife, a parent and a child, an employer and an employee, or a brother and a sister in Christ.

My wife, Susie, and I have been married nearly a quarter of a century. There have been times when I have been insensitive and times (only a few, I hope) when I have spoken harshly. But she has always forgiven me and forgotten the transgression.

We have raised our daughters to young adulthood, and we have made our share of mistakes as parents. But the girls have always forgiven us. There have been moments when they did not always obey, but they later apologized. Together we would always put the incident behind us.

My associate, David Hamilton, and I have worked together for twenty years. We have had sharp disagreements and hurt each other's feelings. But we have always forgiven each other, and in doing so, we continued to move on to a higher level of relationship.

Unfortunately, many relationships with so much potential are destroyed by a refusal to forgive. When people cannot bring it upon themselves to swallow their pride and forgive another or ask for forgiveness, they are building barriers in place of bridges to better relationships. Forgiving and forgetting are keys to every happy marriage, productive business career, and lasting friendship.

Going Home

Paul continues his treatise to Philemon with determined words about burying the hatchet. He writes, "I am sending him [Onesimus] back" (v. 12).

As I have previously mentioned, Onesimus had been working for Philemon, but he had illegally run away, ending up in Rome. It is strongly implied that he had also stolen from

Philemon. Now, after Paul has led Onesimus to Christ, he is sending him back to Colosse, back to Philemon's house.

What do you suppose was Philemon's initial reaction to these words? Was he disgusted? Had he long since planned Onesimus's punishment? Here, finally, was the chance to carry it out. And at the very least, here was an opportunity for some good old-fashioned resentment.

Philemon had been wronged by a trusted servant. If he didn't do anything about it, what would people think of him? And would other servants be encouraged to defy their masters?

As for Onesimus, perhaps he was stealing glances at the letter over Paul's shoulder as he wrote (if he could read, of course). When he found out Paul's intentions, was there a knot in his stomach?

He knew what his punishment could be. The day he confronted Philemon could have been his last one, but Onesimus had to trust that Philemon would forgive. Now that Christ had transformed his life, he had no other option. He was going back.

Both of the men needed Paul, and the encouragement that he had to offer, to propel them toward taking the necessary steps toward reconciliation.

What did it take to bring the two sides together and to mend the broken relationship? The same thing that it takes today. To begin with, the offending person must come to the table not only with contrite words but also with a repentant heart, that is, changed behavior. Without the person's willingness to do things differently and make up for wrongdoing, there will be no genuine healing of the friendship.

In the Old Testament book of 1 Samuel, a young wife named Abigail took it upon herself to ask for forgiveness for something that was not even her fault. She is described as "a woman of good understanding" (25:3).

Abigail's husband, Nabal, was a wealthy owner of many sheep and goats. First Samuel 25 reports that he "was harsh and evil in his doings" (v. 3). David and his army of men had watched over Nabal's flocks and servants, protecting them from any potential outside harm.

After a few months, David sent messengers to Nabal to ask for provisions for the men who had stood guard. Nabal rudely rebuffed the messengers, and in response to such treatment, David set out with four hundred men to slay every male in Nabal's household.

When Abigail heard of the impending disaster, she immediately ordered her servants to load a generous supply of food on donkeys. Then she mounted a donkey and went out to meet David. When she saw him, she quickly dismounted and fell on her face in front of David, asking his forgiveness on behalf of her husband.

David's heart was softened, and he answered her, "Blessed is your advice and blessed are you, because you have kept me this day . . . from avenging myself with my own hand. . . . Go up in peace to your house. See, I have heeded your voice" (vv. 33, 35).

Abigail succeeded in her quest for forgiveness because she acted quickly, sincerely, and humbly. She was also generous in making amends, probably giving more than David would have expected in the first place.

When You've Offended Others

In a strained relationship each of us has a tendency to feel wronged. But so does the other person! That is exactly why some of us live a lifetime with broken friendships.

Few of us want to take personal responsibility and to admit that we are the offender. We have been programmed since childhood to point the finger at someone else.

But could there be a little of Onesimus in all of us? Could it be that we have something to learn from him today regarding mending broken relationships?

Are you an Onesimus? Do you need to admit you were wrong, whereas before you insisted you were right? What might you need to say or do in order to remedy a situation?

Some things can never be completely erased, such as hurtful words, actions, and neglect of a relationship. But we are expected to make things right to the extent that we are able.

Suppose I throw a ball through your living room window. "Oh, I'm so sorry!" I exclaim. "Well, these things happen!" How are you going to feel if I make no effort to pay for or restore the damage?

Many instances in Scripture describe how the offending person is to pay back even more than was taken. After lunch with Jesus one day, the swindling tax collector Zacchaeus burst out of his house, telling the world, in effect, "I'm giving half of what I own to the poor, and if I've cheated anybody, I'll pay back four times the amount" (Luke 19:8). When the heart is truly changed, we want to do everything possible to set things right.

The Greek word for repentance literally means "to change one's mind." Onesimus has changed his mind about his actions of the past and is now on his way back to make amends.

He is not on his way home to argue his case. Some of us go back to others in hopes of reconciliation, only to find ourselves still trying to justify past behavior and prove ourselves right. Not Onesimus. He is taking responsibility for what he has done. He is repentant. He needs forgiveness, and so Paul is asking Philemon to open his heart and forgive.

Be Reconciled to Others

Some of us in estranged relationships have resigned ourselves to the belief that we will live out our days without reconciliation. That is unnecessary and against God's will for our lives.

Matthew 5:23–24 speaks about this issue: "Therefore if you bring your gift to the altar, and there remember that your brother has something against you, leave your gift there before the altar, and go your way. First be reconciled to your brother, and then come and offer your gift."

The altar gifts were more often than not offerings of meat. Meat does not keep for long, especially out in the open air. These verses tell us how quickly we are expected to make things right with others.

There might be a different ending to our story had Onesimus received counsel from some "professionals" today instead of from Paul. Some today would have listened to his story and offered him this counsel: "Look, forget about your past. You can find justification in what you did. Go on with your life. Try to learn from your mistakes. Forget Philemon."

And had Onesimus taken this advice, he would have lived out the rest of his life like some do today, with something left unfinished, with a dark cloud hanging over his head. That is no way to a happy and productive existence.

Could this be the point of frustration with some of us? We are trying to go on with our lives, but something is left undone.

We have not returned with genuine remorse to say, "I am sorry. I was wrong." It may be that until we go back, we will spend our days running into dead ends or zooming around traffic circles instead of making forward progress on the freeways of life.

Only Hollywood movies can be successful with the principle that "love means never having to say you're sorry." In real life, no relationships can succeed on that premise. Those who enjoy the most profitable long-term relationships are the ones who know what it is to say, "I am sorry. Please forgive me."

Onesimus gives us hope. Look at him before you become convinced that your particular case is impossible. There is hope for any of us who will admit that we have failed and want to start over. When we do, we join Onesimus in some pretty good company.

Moses, the emancipator of the Israelites from Egypt, was a murderer. But he heard God's call while in hiding, and he paid attention to it. Going back to Egypt, he led his people to the Promised Land.

King David stole the affection of another man's wife, got her pregnant, and even orchestrated her husband's death. But later, plagued with remorse, he genuinely repented of his actions. To see his sincerity, we need only to read his fifty-first psalm.

When we go back, God forgives. And when God forgives, He remembers our sins no more.

Keep Your Motives Pure

Paul proceeds with his letter: "But without your consent I wanted to do nothing, that your good deed might not be by compulsion, as it were, but voluntary" (v. 14).

As already noted, Paul could have ordered the two to mend

the broken relationship. He could have pulled his apostolic rank on them. But he was wise enough to realize there can be no true reconciliation that is manipulated or forced. It must be voluntary. It must come from a willing heart.

Some persons want to orchestrate reconciliations with hidden agendas for their own self-profit and pride. Reconciliations that last, though, are not forced; they come from a heart with pure motives. Hatchets are never completely buried unless they are done so voluntarily.

Your Folly Becomes His Glory

Paul continues by writing, "For perhaps he departed for a while for this purpose, that you might receive him forever" (v. 15).

What an encouraging thought! Something good can result even from bad experiences.

The sentence begins with the thought-provoking word *perhaps*. Paul is not being presumptuous with this word. He is simply allowing room for something good to emerge out of what began as something bad. He is saying, "Just think about it for a moment. Maybe it happened for a reason."

God revealed a powerful truth through his prophet Isaiah when He said,

> *For My thoughts are not your thoughts,*
> *Nor are your ways My ways. . . .*
> *For as the heavens are higher than the earth,*
> *So are My ways higher than your ways*
> *And My thoughts than your thoughts. (Isa. 55:8–9)*

Is it possible that there is a "perhaps" in your own experience?

The process of mending broken relationships can be a productive learning experience that ultimately results in your own good and God's glory.

When we read the words of verse 15, we are reminded of the story of Joseph and his estrangement from his brothers. Most of us know the story well. Joseph's brothers, filled with jealousy and resentment, sold him to some nomads in a caravan en route to Egypt. They then soaked his beautiful coat in blood and showed it to their father, leading him to believe that Joseph had been killed by a wild animal.

From the human standpoint, most of what happened to Joseph was bad. He was sold as a slave to foreigners, was separated from the father who loved him, and was falsely accused after standing up for his beliefs. A very human reaction would have been for him to spend his undeserved prison time nursing a grudge and planning revenge.

He did neither of these things, however. Instead, it appears that he made the most of his time and talents while in Egypt, and he exerted his energies toward helping others. His faith in God's care and guidance was real.

Through an amazing series of events, Joseph went from prison to the palace, and eventually he became prime minister of the most powerful nation in the world by the time he was thirty years of age.

Famine came to Israel, and Joseph's brothers went to Egypt in hopes of finding food. The brothers' actions had been unconscionable. Joseph was the wounded one. The rift in the relationship had gone on for years and years, but the brothers were repentant. How would he respond after having been wronged by those closest to him?

When Joseph was reunited with his brothers, he said, "But now, do not therefore be grieved nor angry with yourselves because you sold me here; for God sent me before you to preserve life. . . . So now it was not you who sent me here, but God" (Gen. 45:5, 8).

God allowed it. And for a reason. Paul is hoping the same will happen with Philemon and Onesimus. He is setting the stage for what he hopes will be a beautiful reconciliation.

From Slave to Brother

Paul continues his appeal to Philemon by asking him to take Onesimus back, "no longer as a slave but more than a slave—a beloved brother, especially to me but how much more to you, both in the flesh and in the Lord" (v. 16).

Just as a broken bone heals to be stronger than it was before, so is there often a deeper relationship after reconciliation has occurred. The person who was wronged does not soon forget the humility and repentance of the one who mistreated him or her. And the one who committed the offense appreciates the forgiving heart of the person who was hurt.

Philemon needs to have a receptive heart toward Onesimus. His treatment of him "as a beloved brother" will change their relationship forever. This will take enormous strength and humility on Philemon's part, but Paul is confident that he is capable of it.

The new and closer relationship we can enjoy with one another through Jesus Christ does not free us from previous obligations and responsibilities. We are to make things right insofar as it is possible. But Paul is opening Philemon's eyes to a totally new relationship. On the spiritual level Onesimus and Philemon would become equals, "brothers."

Our relationships are transformed when they are changed from within by the love and power we find in being connected to our Source, Jesus Christ.

Leonardo da Vinci, the famous artist known for painting *The Last Supper*, learned a powerful lesson on the importance of mending strained relationships. While most of us are familiar with his famous painting of our Lord's last meal in the Upper Room, few have ever heard the story behind the story.

While in the process of painting his masterpiece, da Vinci had a bitter disagreement with a fellow painter. The master was so enraged that he began to plot an evil scheme. He would paint the face of his adversary into the face of Judas and thus portray him for all posterity as the traitor.

As soon as da Vinci finished painting Judas, everyone immediately recognized him as Leonardo's former friend. He continued to paint the scene, adding each of the disciples into the portrait. It then was time to paint the face of Christ.

As much as he tried, one attempt after another, he could not paint the Lord's face. Something was keeping him from it. His own heart revealed to him that his hatred for his fellow painter was the problem. So, he reconciled with his friend, and repainted Judas's face with another. Then with great liberty, da Vinci painted the face of Christ, completing the masterpiece admired down through the centuries.

Getting Past the Resentment

The problem with some of us who are offended is not that we retaliate but that we harbor resentment. And the truth is, this feeling is much more deadly. The most devastating effect of resentment is not what it does to others but what it does to us.

It will damage us physically. Hatred in the heart can have a damaging effect on such things as blood pressure and normal bodily functions. Many who have been eaten up with resentment have also soon found they were eaten up with ulcers as well.

Resentment has a depressing effect on us mentally. When it consumes us, it can warp our capacity to think rightly. Many people suffer from mental and emotional problems because they are bitter toward others and have never forgiven past wrongs, even though the transgressors have returned in genuine remorse.

But there is more. It also debilitates us spiritually. None of us can be in right relationship with God when we hate or resent someone else.

In another letter, Paul challenges his friends at Ephesus to "let all bitterness, wrath, anger, clamor, and evil speaking be put away from you, with all malice. And be kind to one another, tenderhearted, forgiving one another, even as God in Christ forgave you" (Eph. 4:31–32).

In our macho world a lot of people have a warped image of the person who forgives and forgets and begins again. The caricature in the minds of many is one who is weak and wimpy. However, just the opposite is true. Forgiveness is a positive and powerful force, and it takes a strong person to forgive.

Anyone can be unforgiving. It doesn't take any courage or strength at all. But it takes a strong man or woman to say, "I forgive you. And what is more, I will forget it."

It also takes a strong person to ask for forgiveness. But if you've done someone wrong, you have no other choice.

Pledge today to make things right. Take back the Onesimus

in your life. Make a call to the Philemon you've been avoiding. Bury the hatchet with your brother. Extend a warm hand to your estranged sister in Christ.

Begin again. Start fresh.

Bury the hatchet!

CHAPTER NINE

THE HAND OF FORGIVENESS

*T*HINK FOR A MOMENT about the individuals who have had the greatest impact on your life. As I think about it, four or five people surface in my mind. My dad and mom are two of them. They surrounded me with love. They instilled self-confidence within me, causing me to believe my reach could always exceed my grasp. I never remember them missing one of my ball games. They were always there for me.

I think of my wife, Susie. No one knows quite like I what an incredible individual she really is. For over twenty years we have been "one"—physically, emotionally, spiritually, parentally—in the most wonderful sense imaginable.

My mentor, Fred Swank, comes quickly to mind. He was a people person extraordinaire. He was like a second father to me. He loved me and gave me his most valuable possession, his time. Although he is no longer with us physically, a day seldom goes by that I do not put into practice something he taught me about relationships.

As I think about these people, the thought dawns on me that they all have one thing in common. It isn't just that they believed in me and encouraged me. But each, in his or her own way, forgave me of my faults. All of them forgot my shortcomings.

There were more times than I like to remember when I rebelled against my father. But he always forgave me and never brought it up again. As many times as I have let Susie down, she has always forgiven me and forgotten it. The same holds true with Dr. Swank. I made a lot of mistakes under his tutorship and supervision, but he always forgave me and helped me learn from those very mistakes so they wouldn't be made again.

Forgiveness has a dynamic power in the lives of others. There is something about it that brings out the best in us, regardless of whether we are on the giving or receiving end.

We are talking about relationships here. This is what life is all about. The most essential key in ongoing, positive relationships is the ability to forgive. In fact, the strongest lifetime relationships are between those who know what it is to repent and forgive and forget.

The Value of a Friend

Paul gives a wealth of encouragement on forgiving others and restoring broken relationships in another of his letters. During the same year that he wrote to Philemon, he penned a letter to all the Christians in Colosse, where Philemon lived. Maybe he even had this particular situation in mind in Colossians 3:12–14:

> *Therefore, as the elect of God, holy and beloved, put on tender mercies, kindness, humility, meekness, longsuffering; bearing with one another, and forgiving one another, if anyone has a complaint against another; even as*

Christ forgave you, so you also must do. But above all these things put on love, which is the bond of perfection.

These words undoubtedly had a positive effect on Philemon's attitude toward the man who had wronged him.

We live in a day when more and more people are going from one relationship to another, leaving strings of broken hearts and battered hopes in their wake. Too few seem to want to really pay the price of making a relationship work.

There are those who, when faced with a breakdown in a relationship, simply junk it. Instead of isolating the problem and making some repairs, they bail out. It doesn't matter how much has been invested in it previously. We don't do this with our automobiles. We invest in a car, and if it doesn't start in the morning, what do we do? Junk it? No! If we can't fix it ourselves, we call for help. We find the problem and get it fixed. The car is too valuable to do anything else.

In the same way, we make too many deposits of love and time in relationships to walk off and leave them when we have trouble getting them going on a particular morning. If we can't fix them ourselves, we shouldn't be too proud to get some help.

In essence, Paul is offering his help in mending the broken relationship between Philemon and Onesimus. He knows the relationship is worth salvaging, and he is intent on getting that across to Philemon. Onesimus wants to be reconciled. He is willing to make the first move.

But Philemon must be willing to do his part. He must be willing to forgive and forget in order to give the relationship a fresh new beginning. If Philemon says that it is all right for

Onesimus to return, yet he remains resentful and retaliatory, there will be no real reconciliation.

Admittedly, forgiving Onesimus was a big pill for Philemon to swallow. In fact, you cannot know how big a pill it is unless you have been deeply wronged by someone you trusted. Philemon had sustained a great financial loss from Onesimus's actions.

Most people would not have batted an eye had he chosen to have Onesimus executed or at least severely punished. Before his relationship with Christ, that would have been the expected course of action. It certainly would have been the human thing to do.

But because Philemon is a fellow believer, Paul has higher hopes and expectations for him. He has faith that Philemon will pay the price and make the adjustments to be in fellowship with Onesimus.

When You've Been Offended

Perhaps you are a Philemon. Someone has lied to you, stolen from you, gossiped about you, or done something worse. All of us are offended by others sooner or later. We can't control who wrongs us, but we can control our attitudes and responses toward them when they do.

Jesus tells us to forgive without limits. Peter came to Him one day, feeling very righteous, and asked, "Lord, how often shall my brother sin against me, and I forgive him? Up to seven times?" Surely, that number was over and above the call of duty. The Jews taught that the requirement was three times. How shocked Peter must have been when Jesus answered, "I do not say to you, up to seven times, but up to seventy times seven" (Matt. 18:21–22).

Even more sobering is this blunt statement of Jesus: "For if you forgive men their trespasses, your heavenly Father will also forgive you. But if you do not forgive men their trespasses, neither will your Father forgive your trespasses" (Matt. 6:14–15).

Forgiving seems difficult to do when our focus is on what has been done to us. But when we consider the magnitude of our offenses toward God, the way He has forgiven us, and what He had to go through to do it, it becomes easier.

Charlene is a good example. She struggled with forgiving her husband for having an affair. It was all she could do to look him in the eyes or stand in the same room with him. During the entire ordeal, he showed no sign of remorse. Eventually, he walked out on her for good.

"I couldn't get past it for a year and a half," she confided, "and I spent precious time and energy figuring out how to get even with him."

During that difficult period, a friend led Charlene to Christ, and the transformation in her life was amazing. "I realized," she said, "that the extent of my spiritual adultery toward God was just as bad as what Tom had done. I'm not excusing him, but it is easier to start forgiving him because I know I've been forgiven of just as much."

Forgiving Is Never Easy

During His days on earth, Jesus became a powerful model of true Christian forgiveness. He was constantly being unfairly accused and attacked, but His agenda was to get out God's message of love and forgiveness to a lost world. We don't get the impression that He took offenses personally—rather He considered the sources!

111

His most dramatic statement of forgiveness came from the cross as He asked God to forgive the ones who were putting Him to death. With pain writhing through His broken body, He looked to the heavens and said, "Father, forgive them, for they do not know what they do" (Luke 23:34).

Author Max Lucado penned some beautiful thoughts about these words in one of his classic books:

> *How Jesus, with a body racked with pain, eyes blinded by his own blood, and lungs yearning for air, could speak on behalf of some heartless thugs is beyond my comprehension. Never, never have I seen such love. If ever a person deserved a shot at revenge, Jesus did. But he didn't take it. Instead he died for them. How could he do it? I don't know. But I do know that all of a sudden my wounds seem very painless. My grudges and hard feelings are suddenly childish.*[1]

Forgiving others when they've wronged us is not an easy thing to do. It's difficult to turn the other cheek (see Matt. 5:39). It's hard to bless others when they've cursed us (see Matt. 5:44). It's unnatural to swallow our pride, stick out a hand, and offer forgiveness when we've been wronged.

But it's what Jesus modeled. And it's what God expects.

Corrie ten Boom saw more than her share of troubles. She was wronged more than most of us can even imagine. And she knew what it was to wrestle with trying to forgive.

As a young woman during World War Two, Corrie and her sister Betsie were found to be hiding Jews in their home. They were arrested, interrogated, and sent to Ravensbruck, an infamous German concentration camp. There her sister Betsie died. Corrie lived to tell her story in the best-selling book *The Hiding Place.*

She relates that years after the atrocities she was invited to speak at a church in Munich. There she came face-to-face with the former Nazi who stood watch at the shower door in the processing center at Ravensbruck. She had never forgotten his face.

Suddenly, it all flashed back—the room full of mocking, jeering men; the heaps of clothing piled in the corner; and Betsie's pained and tormented face.

The man approached her with a radiant smile at the conclusion of the service. "How grateful I am for your message, Fraulein. To think that, as you say, He [Jesus] has washed my sins away!" he said.

The man offered his hand in greeting, but Corrie ten Boom, who had spoken so often of the need to love and forgive, kept her own hand at her side. Vengeful and angry thoughts flooded her mind.

She writes, "Jesus Christ had died for this man; was I going to ask for more? Lord Jesus, I prayed, forgive me and help me to forgive him."

Corrie ten Boom tried to smile at the man. But she could not. She struggled to extend her hand. She could not. She felt nothing. No love. No warmth. She then breathed a silent prayer: "Jesus, I cannot forgive him. Give me your forgiveness." As she took the man's hand, an incredible thing happened. Into her heart leaped a love for this stranger that was overpowering.[2]

Corrie discovered that it is no more on our own forgiveness

than it is on our own goodness that the world's healing hinges. Along with Christ's commands to forgive others, He gives the strength and love to do so.

The Mark of a Christian

What Paul was asking of Philemon and Onesimus was no small task. He was calling on those children of God to do things that would clearly push the limits of their human faith and abilities. He knew that they would not be able to reconcile on their own. They needed encouragement. They needed time. And they needed the strength that only Christ can bring.

By asking those things of Philemon and Onesimus, Paul was trying to get across a powerful and timeless truth to them: genuine faith must be accompanied by positive, caring behavior. A true follower of Christ will always act on faith through sincere love and forgiveness and compassion. Both Philemon and Onesimus must put the past behind and move forward if they are sincere in wanting to do what is right in the eyes of God.

The same holds true for you and me. God's love and forgiveness are gifts we could never repay. And it's a good thing for us that He doesn't ask us to. But they are not gifts we should take for granted.

If someone has wronged you, forgive the person. If you've wronged someone else, ask forgiveness. Don't think of the things that happened or the things that could happen when you meet; just do what you know is right. Make that call. Write that letter. Give back what isn't yours. Get over the grudge. Get past the pain and guilt and anger.

We will never find true joy and contentment in our relationship with God until we first make things right with others.

We All Need Forgiveness

There is a deeper story here than just the relationships between Paul, Philemon, and Onesimus. What we really have is a picture of the way we can become reconciled to the Source of power for living.

In a sense, we are all Onesimus. We are all the offending party. The Creator made us to fellowship with Him, but we chose to go our own way and leave Him out of our lives. We stole what is rightfully His—our allegiance, our obedience, and our love. We took them and left.

He is the offended party. He provided a perfect paradise for us all, giving us security and direction. But we thought we could do better. He then gave the best He had to offer, and we nailed Him to a cross of execution.

Christ has paid our debt of sin for us, and we are accepted at the throne of God—not on the basis of what we have done but on the basis of what Christ has done and who He is. He has a relationship with God and stands in the gap for us. Jesus came into the world to take you and me by one of His nail-pierced hands. Then He reached up to His Father with the other and brought us into a relationship with Him.

Likewise, Paul has a relationship with Philemon and bridges the gap between him and Onesimus. He offers to pay Onesimus's debt.

What would be the outcome if Onesimus threw away Paul's letter on the way home and decided instead to plead his case by himself? What would his reception be like back at

Colosse? And what would his final destiny be in Philemon's household?

In the same way, what will be the outcome if we try to go to God on our own merit, tossing aside Jesus' "letter of recommendation" for us? What will our reception be like on the Day of Judgment? And what will our final destiny be?

Is there an Onesimus reading these words? God is ready and waiting to receive you. He wants to forgive. And what is more, He will also forget.

Christ will recommend you to Him if you will let Him. He will present your case. He may be saying to you right now, even through the words of this book, "Let's bury the hatchet. Let's start over. Let's have a new beginning."

And the beautiful truth is, He has already buried the hatchet deep into a Roman cross outside the city wall of Jerusalem almost two thousand years ago. There He demonstrated His love and receptive heart toward us in reconciliation.

One New Year's Day I stood at that very spot called Skull Hill. The largest snowfall in decades covered the landscape of Jerusalem. It was beautiful as it nestled in the crevices on the face of the mountain.

The holes that look like eye sockets and make Golgotha different in appearance from any other hill on earth were filled with snow. And then, the words of the prophet Isaiah came quickly to mind:

> *"Come now, and let us reason together,"*
> *Says the LORD,*
> *"Though your sins are like scarlet,*
> *They shall be as white as snow." (1:18)*

Come home to Him as Onesimus came home to Philemon. He wants to take you back. He wants to forgive and forget. But the first move is up to you.

Let today be the day that you begin the greatest journey of your life—the journey back home, where you belong.

Crossing the Rubicon

If then you count me as a partner, receive him as you would me. But if he has wronged you or owes anything, put that on my account. I, Paul, am writing with my own hand. I will repay—not to mention to you that you owe me even your own self besides. Yes, brother, let me have joy from you in the Lord; refresh my heart in the Lord. Having confidence in your obedience, I write to you, knowing that you will do even more than I say.
—Philemon 17–21

CHAPTER TEN

BUILDING BRIDGES
OF COMMITMENT

*T*HE YEAR WAS 49 B.C. An order came down to Julius Caesar to disband his army and give up the struggle to conquer Rome. He stood on the banks of the Rubicon River and pondered his dilemma.

If he gave up the fight, all of the previous efforts would have been for nothing. If he defied orders and failed, the results would be disastrous. But if he crossed the river, there could be no turning back.

Finally, he made the decision. Caesar discarded his orders, turned to his troops, and led his dedicated legion across the Rubicon to march against Rome. This act of commitment to his cause paved the way for him to become ruler of the Roman world.

Since that day the phrase "crossing the Rubicon" has been used to signify total commitment to a cause from which there can be no turning back.

There is a Rubicon in every interpersonal relationship. There is a line of commitment we cross after which we are "in" for the duration.

A man and a woman may date for years, but when they stand at the marriage altar and say, "I do," there is no turning back. They must make the best of their lives together.

A couple may enjoy a carefree life without the responsibility of children, going where they please when they please, and spending extra money on enjoyments for themselves. But when they have a baby, everything changes. The child's welfare depends on their sacrificial commitment.

Someone may own a business and answer to no other person when it comes to making the decisions for that company. But if he signs a contract for a partnership, it's no longer business as usual. Someone else's wishes, ideas, and future must be considered.

Every day someone crosses the Rubicon of relationships. And the success of the relationship depends on the level of commitment—the willingness to move forward and never look back. It's a test of the friendship. It's a test of sincerity. But most of all, it's a test of character.

Commitment is a lost word in the vocabulary of many relationships today. Some married people are committed, but only to their own happiness and comfort. Thus, they move to another relationship when their satisfaction wanes. They promise to stay with it, but when the going gets tough, they bail out.

Many profess a commitment at the office, but they are really committed to their own personal advancement. Loyalty to the company is nonexistent. They see no farther than the next paycheck, and the minute a better offer comes, they're out the door.

Some have trouble committing to their children. They are willing to feed and clothe them and give them the little spare time they have. But when it comes time for some personal or professional sacrifices, they balk at the thought. If they must choose between time at the office and time with the kids, the children usually lose. Many parents are committed—but only to a point.

Staying Faithful to Your Friends

Paul, having already addressed such vital principles as encouragement, forgiveness, and acceptance, now turns his attention to the importance of allegiance to each other.

He expresses his commitment to Onesimus when he writes Philemon and says, "If then you count me as a partner, receive him as you would me. But if he has wronged you or owes anything, put that on my account" (vv. 17–18).

Paul will now vouch for Onesimus. Yes, Onesimus has a terrible reputation in his hometown of Colosse, but Paul wants him to have a fresh start. He cares more about Onesimus's future than his past.

Do you know anyone who has really blown it in a public way? Not the woman who is impatient with her family behind closed doors, or the guy who spends too much money on clothes, but someone who has started tongues wagging.

"Couldn't they have waited until the wedding? . . . Joe has at least two more years behind bars if he behaves himself. Wonder if he has that temper under control? . . . It's not surprising that some of the money stuck to her fingers; I've always had my doubts about her. . . . What was Onesimus thinking? Did he really think he would get away with it?"

What is your attitude toward these humiliated fellow human beings? Are you one of the tongue waggers, making sure that the news is out? Or are you a helper who makes direct, healing contact with them in a way that changes their lives forever?

Risky Business

Reaching out to others is risky business. Sometimes they rebuff us and our efforts. It becomes safer to put up a barrier or at least to don a mask than to reach out.

Genuine commitment to another means being able to do the right thing by the person, even when it means risking rejection.

Reaching out a helping hand is easier when we remember our sinfulness, and that Christ stooped down and rescued us from ourselves. He did this even when we didn't deserve it and in the face of extreme ingratitude. Jesus risks rejection in reaching out to others. We must be willing to do the same if we are to lift up someone else and perhaps even make a new friend.

Alan Loy McGinnis discusses the importance of being able to handle rejection if we are to find success in our lives and our relationships:

> I once talked to a sales manager who had coached some of the most successful and best-paid marketing executives in the business.
>
> "Do you know what is the most telltale sign that a man will be a good salesman?" he asked.
>
> I guessed. "Intelligence? Ambition? Good looks?"
>
> All were wrong.
>
> "It's his ability to handle rejection," the man said. "If he is cowed by failure with a few customers, he'll never hit the big time. But if he can endure rejection and keep trying,

confident that he will eventually find a customer where everything clicks, there is no stopping that man."

The same principle works in our close relationships. Our ability to discover love will in part depend on our ability to handle rejection. Once in a while someone will spurn us. When we initiate a friendship and the other does not wish it, that rejection can burn through many layers of skin.

But the inescapable fact is that not everyone will like you. When they do not, it is not necessarily a reflection on you. The chemistry simply was not right.[1]

Building Bridges

As we go through life relating to others, we do one of two things. We build bridges, or we build barriers. If we build more bridges than barriers, we will have more loyal and committed friends. If we build mostly walls, few will be able to cross over with us.

Russell is a good example of this. At fifty years of age, he has gone most of his life without committing deeply to anyone or anything. No one is allowed to get close to him. In his late twenties he fathered a child with his girlfriend. She assumed they would get married, but he never asked. He also played little or no role in raising his daughter. Eventually, his girlfriend gave up and married someone else. Russell was virtually left out of his daughter's life.

The military drafted him during the war and offered him a good career afterward, but he took a discharge at the first opportunity. "I just hated being confined," he explained.

He then took his entitlements and put them toward a college education. But after graduation, he couldn't hold down a job.

He bounced from company to company until finally his poor reputation caught up with him. Nobody wanted a job-hopper like Russell.

The offers for work became more menial as the days went by. Today, Russell works as a night custodian in an office building. The hours are long and the pay is low, and he is counting the days until something better comes along. Chances are good that he'll quit in the near future.

Though he had several chances to marry, he never did. Over half his life is over, and he is still sad and lonely and unsuccessful.

Russell's story is a tragic but common one. Too many people today are afraid to commit, to be vulnerable, to risk getting hurt in relationships. So they keep to themselves, never trying to get close to anyone.

Are there any bridges being built on the construction site of your relationships? I'm not talking about letting anyone and everyone cross over into the hidden things of the heart. I'm not referring to being indiscriminate in what you share.

Openness with others is not a call for us to reveal all the details of our hidden secrets. We need our private places. I'm talking about bridges here, not interstate highways. I'm speaking of being vulnerable and taking the risk of opening up with someone else.

Something wonderful happens when two people connect in openness and honesty. Openness has its own way of building a bridge.

Jesus' openness made Him attractive to others. He was transparent. He traveled with His friends, ate with them, prayed with them, and wept with them.

Jesus was a people person. He cared about their struggles.

He built bridges of commitment across which others could walk with Him. He allowed people to look into His heart and to know Him. He told others of His own needs. And though it was risky because some rejected Him, many others opened up to this One who had made it so easy to reach Him.

Mary, Martha, and Lazarus were among the people who knew Jesus best. They saw Him in every situation—helping people, resting and relaxing, and praying. Mary and Martha knew that He cried when Lazarus died. His openness and vulnerability were bridges to their relationship with Him.

When we are transparent with others, they are encouraged to relax and to share themselves with us. Establishing successful and meaningful relationships demands a mutual vulnerability.

Taking the Risk

Ironically, the things we usually try to keep hidden from others are often the very things that would attract them to us. If we could only open up and share ourselves, we'd find that we're not that much different from others.

Everyone has fears. Everyone is afraid of being hurt by someone else in a relationship. Those who are able to get over those fears have learned a valuable lesson somewhere along the way: you have to risk getting hurt if you ever want to get close. It's the only way to develop meaningful relationships with others.

My own experience is a good example. Growing up, I came from rather humble origins. We were far from wealthy. My background brought little status to my career.

For a while I considered this a hindrance to my future and my relationships. I wondered what others might think of me and whether they might look down on me. It sounds foolish now, but in my immaturity I sometimes tried to pretend to be someone I wasn't.

When I became open with others about my background, I found that what I thought was a problem was, in reality, an asset. People didn't look down on me; rather, they respected me all the more for what I had achieved.

We never have to be afraid of the truth.

More Than a Friend

As Paul writes to Philemon, he chooses an interesting Greek word in calling him a "partner." It is a word describing one mutually shared life. Paul and Philemon were connected. They were "together" because of their shared life in Christ. Being partners gave them a sense of mutual obligation for the well-being of fellow Christians, specifically Onesimus in this case.

Those who are committed to others sense an obligation to look after their best interests. This principle is beautifully illustrated in the Old Testament book of Ruth.

Ruth was a Moabite widow of an Israelite man. Her husband had died in Moab, and her mother-in-law, Naomi, was returning to Israel in search of a better life. On the road home, Naomi turned to her two daughters-in-law and told them to go back to their people. One of them did, but Ruth determined to stay with Naomi. Ruth's declaration of commitment, fidelity, and love is one of the best-known passages in Scripture:

> *Entreat me not to leave you,*
> *Or to turn back from following after you;*
> *For wherever you go, I will go;*

And wherever you lodge, I will lodge;
Your people shall be my people,
And your God, my God.
Where you die, I will die,
And there will I be buried.
The LORD do so to me, and more also,
If anything but death parts you and me. (Ruth 1:16–17)

Because of her commitment to Naomi and because she fulfilled her sense of obligation to her, circumstances worked so that Ruth was privileged to be an ancestor of Jesus Christ.

Above the Call of Duty

The journey back to a right relationship can be arduous enough. But it can be made more difficult by those who are not ready and eager to forgive and forget. Since Paul has already referred to Onesimus as "my own heart" (v. 12), Philemon's rejection of Onesimus would be like a rejection of Paul.

Paul knows that Philemon has been cheated, and he feels obliged to see that the situation is rectified. He is willing to take care of this problem himself.

He continues the letter, "If he has done you any wrong or owes you anything, charge it to me. I, Paul, am writing this with my own hand. I will pay it back" (vv. 18–19 NIV).

Paul instructs Philemon to "charge" whatever is owed him by Onesimus to his own account. Paul is in no way suggesting that Philemon forget about Onesimus's past wrongs or ignore the debt. Instead, he writes a promissory note with his own hand. Many scholars believe that it was a legally binding document in that day.

Something beautiful is happening in the relationship between Paul and Onesimus. Paul is offering to pay a debt he doesn't owe. Why? Because Onesimus owes a debt he cannot pay, and Paul cares about him!

This willingness to pay the debt of someone else has its roots in love and in our relationship with God.

Martin Luther said, "We are all God's Onesimi." We, like him, have gone our own way in rebellion against the One who loves us most. The Bible refers to what we owe our Source as a "sin debt." We cannot pay it. And we are separated from our most important relationship because of it. Just as Paul had nothing to do with Onesimus's guilt, neither does Christ with ours.

And yet, just as Paul assumed the debt he did not owe, so Jesus made His way across His own Rubicon to a Roman cross to pay our debt. In essence, He said to His Father about you and me what Paul said to Philemon about Onesimus: "If he has done you any wrong or owes you anything, charge it to me. . . . I will pay it back."

Because of this, those of us who have trusted in Christ will be accepted by God when we present ourselves before His throne. In the same way, Paul's letter will pave the way for Onesimus's acceptance by Philemon.

Isaiah said,

> *All we like sheep have gone astray;*
> *We have turned, every one, to his own way;*
> *And the LORD has laid on Him the iniquity of us all.*
> *(53:6)*

130

Those who have connected with the Source through Jesus Christ can go to the computer in heaven, pull up their names, look at their accounts, and read the words, "Paid in full!"

The bridge has been built. And it will stand for eternity.

CHAPTER ELEVEN

A FRIEND
TO THE END

RELATIONSHIPS STAND STRONG through the years when friends stick up for each other. I remember an experience in my own life when I was falsely accused and a friend rose to my defense. Although we have been separated from that experience by hundreds of miles and many years, I have never forgotten it. My friend and I have a deep bond between us as a result.

How much more do you think Onesimus was committed to Paul after he got wind of the fact that Paul had risen so strongly to his defense? And how much more would your friends be committed to you if you proved beyond a doubt your devotion to them?

Writer and lecturer Landon Saunders asks, "Isn't it time to make a fresh commitment to keeping our friendships in good repair?" Then he follows that question with some thoughts on what it means to be a true friend to others. In his words, it means saying to those we care for:

Today I'll be a friend—no conditions—no reservations—no

expectations—I will simply be a friend. And nothing my friend does can change that. He doesn't have to follow my script in order to be my friend. Friendship does not grow out of the demands (expectations) I place on others; it grows out of what I am.

In the same vein, what would it do for a marriage for each spouse to know of the other's devotion through thick and thin? Commitment to another person cements a relationship like almost nothing else can.

Saunders poses another question:

Have you asked yourself: "Just how devoted am I, really, to my marriage?" A marriage needs devotion. Without it, the companionship will begin to break down—along with the marriage.

Marriage means a man and a woman looking deeply into each other's eyes and saying: I will never leave you. Others may come and go in your life, but I never will. If you wrinkle, I will love you. If you fail, I will stay with you. If you get sick, I'll feed you, bathe you, sit up with you—anything—except leave you. I will never leave you.[1]

Paul is encouraging Philemon to be a true friend to Onesimus and to himself. He wants Philemon to know the beauty of loyalty and commitment and friendship. He wants him to put the past behind and accept Onesimus as a friend and a brother.

True Loyalty
Paul continues his letter: "If he . . . owes you anything . . . I

will pay it . . . not to mention that you owe me your very self. . . . I do wish, brother, that I may have some benefit from you in the Lord; refresh my heart in Christ" (vv. 18–20 NIV).

Loyal friends get the big picture. They see past themselves to realize the importance of reciprocation. They are quick to return favors.

Bill Hybels speaks eloquently about "expending yourself for your friends" in his book *Who You Are (When No One's Looking)*:

The world does not understand the Christian concept of brotherhood and sisterhood. The world says to find friends among like-minded, like-incomed people who vote like you and have about the same golf handicap. These are safe people; they won't start asking for counseling or financial assistance. If you keep a healthy distance from them, the relationship won't get muddied up with commitments or expectations.

These friendships work until the bottom falls out of your life. You face a pressing problem, a tragic loss or a serious illness, and suddenly you realize that no one cares much about you. You made no investment in anybody else's life, and so now when you need to make a withdrawal, there's no money in the friendship bank.

Christian friendship is different. You find a few brothers and sisters and decide at the outset that you are going to expend yourself for them. You invest time, energy and often money in them. Because you meet regularly and talk, you get into each other's lives. You encourage, counsel, challenge and rebuke each other. You make sacrifices. Some time ago, a close brother wrote me a letter that began, "This letter is in part to tell you formally that whatever I have is yours. If you and your family ever need any kind of help, just say the word." A colleague once told me, "I know I could go to the phone right now and call five friends who would give me a car, a hand, a place to live if I needed it. This is one of the greatest blessings of my life."[2]

Loyalty is a treasured commodity. When you find someone who is loyal to you to the end, who will stick by you no matter what, who will even take your debts and pay them when you're in need, you don't take the friendship for granted. You hang on to the person and respond with the same kind of commitment.

Paul is showing Philemon just how serious he is about his friendship with Onesimus. And in doing so, he is demonstrating the kind of loyalty and friendship he hopes he can expect in return.

Love Without Condition

It is an unfortunate fact that loyalty today is in short supply. Many people seem to be interested only in getting, being on the receiving end of the relationship most of the time. Few are objective enough to see the need for reciprocation, for returning favors and giving of themselves to someone else.

When our daughters were young, we enjoyed taking them to the park. They loved to ride the seesaw. If I close my eyes, I can still see them . . . up and down . . . up and down. Relationships have a similar effect. There are times in a relationship when one of the parties does most of the giving and the other most of the receiving.

Then some circumstances of life come along and turn the tables on us. For a while, the roles are reversed.

Anyone who has been married for a long period of time knows of this law of reciprocation. For example, I know of a wife whose husband recently lost his job. Although he doesn't verbalize it, he is having a real struggle with his self-confidence. He is contentious and on edge, and he says things he doesn't really mean. He is not as affectionate and giving as he once was. The money is dwindling. Fear is setting in.

Quite honestly, the wife is not getting much from the relationship. Some women would allow this frustration to cause them to pull away. Some might even pull out. But this woman realizes her husband needs her unconditional love now more than ever, even though he doesn't deserve it. So she gives. And for a time, she gives much more than she receives.

Committed friends see past themselves and their momentary needs to the importance of reciprocation. They give. They understand that people need friends the most when they do not necessarily deserve them.

The desire to always be receiving and the inability to see that friendship is a two-way street are key factors in the destruction of many relationships.

Jesus said that we are to love others as we love ourselves. He commanded us to treat others the way we want to be treated. If we want others to generously give to us of their time and resources, we must be willing to do the same.

Be a giver. Return a favor. You never know when you might need someone to be there for you in a time of need.

Doing More Than Expected

Paul concludes his paragraph on the importance of commit-ment by saying, "Confident of your obedience, I write to you, knowing that you will do even more than I ask" (v. 21 NIV).

Paul is wise and winsome. He knows how hard it is to feel good about others if we do not feel good about ourselves. He is letting Philemon know, without question, that he believes he will do the right thing.

This optimistic approach has incredible results. It brings out the best in Philemon. We bring out the best in others by letting them know we are confident that they will come through for us.

Committed friends believe the best about each other, and they come through in the clutch. In fact, as Paul reveals, they do more than is expected of them.

Can you imagine Philemon's emotions as he reads this letter from his trusted friend? Paul has dropped the Onesimus bomb, laid out the whole situation, asked for a favor, and offered his own commitment.

Having advocated the position of Philemon's adversary, Paul now affirms his confidence in Philemon with the assurance that he will do even more than he is asked. He lets Philemon know he believes he will do what is right—and all in advance of the fact.

Paul believes in Philemon to the extent that just a few sentences earlier he called on his friend to "welcome him [One-simus] as you would welcome me."

How would Philemon have welcomed Paul? Undoubtedly as an honored guest and friend. There would have been a warm greeting, a washing of Paul's feet (one of Onesimus's old jobs), a hearty meal (that Onesimus would have served), and a conversation between equals.

For Philemon to treat Onesimus this way would have been a mind-boggling, jaw-dropping scenario to the person looking on in Philemon's household. It was an almost impossible request, humanly speaking. But Paul was optimistic. And he shows this by concluding his thoughts with, "Confident of your obedience, I write to you, *knowing* that you will do even more than I ask" (emphasis mine).

Think "Optimism"

Paul could have used two different Greek words to indicate this particular knowledge. One of them refers to a type of knowledge that comes by way of the mind through the senses. This knowledge is grounded in personal experience. It says, "I know because I have experienced it. I have touched it. I have smelled it. I have tasted it. Thus, I know."

The other word is indicative of seeing with the mind's eye. That is, we do not have to experience it to *know* it is true. We just know. This is the word Paul chooses when he lets Philemon "know" that he believes he will do even more than Paul asks.

In essence, he is saying to his friend, "I don't have to see it first. I have confidence in you. I *know* you will do the right thing."

Do your friends and family know you have confidence in them? Or do you always have to experience their performance before believing in them or affirming them in some way?

Susie and I have raised our daughters to young adulthood. Since the day of her birth, there has not been one single day in either girl's life when she did not hear me say, "I am proud to be your dad."

In a thousand ways we have tried to let them know we believe in them. We are confident they will do the right things in life, and in fact, we know they will do even more than we ask. Letting others know you believe in them brings out the best in them far more readily than berating them over their shortcomings.

Paul does not order or coerce Philemon to receive Onesimus. It is Philemon's choice. Loyalty and commitment must be voluntary if they are to be genuine. Thus, he simply presents his case, expresses his confidence in both parties, and leaves the ball in Philemon's court.

He knows that people have a way of becoming what we encourage them to be, not what we compel them to be. Expecting the best in others and expressing confidence in them to do more than is expected go a long way in helping them to do the right thing.

That's the beauty of optimism and encouragement. When people see that we believe in them, that we notice their good traits, they usually rise to the occasion. More than that, they exceed our expectations.

Author and humorist Art Buchwald writes of an interesting experience he had while spending a day with an eternal optimist. His friend was intent on changing the mood of New York with nothing but a smile and an attitude of believing the best about others. Here is how Buchwald describes the event:

> I was in New York the other day and rode with a friend in a taxi. When we got out, my friend said to the driver, "Thank you for the ride. You did a superb job of driving."

The taxi driver was stunned for a second. Then he said, "Are you a wise guy or something?"

"No, my dear man, and I'm not putting you on. I admire the way you keep cool in heavy traffic."

"Yeah," the driver said and drove off.

"What was that all about?" I asked.

"I am trying to bring love back to New York," he said. "I believe it's the only thing that can save the city."

"How can one man save New York?"

"It's not one man. I believe I have made that taxi driver's day. Suppose he has 20 fares. He's going to be nice to those 20 fares because someone was nice to him. Those fares in turn will be kinder to their employees or shopkeepers or waiters or even their own families. Eventually the goodwill could spread to at least 1,000 people. Now that isn't bad, is it?"

We were walking past a structure in the process of being built and passed five workmen eating their lunch. My friend stopped. "That's a magnificent job you men have done. It must be difficult and dangerous work."

The workmen eyed my friend suspiciously.

"When will it be finished?"

"June," a man grunted.

"Ah. That really is impressive. You must all be very proud."

We walked away. I said to him, "I haven't seen anyone like you since *Man of La Mancha*."

"When those men digest my words, they will feel better for it. Somehow the city will benefit from their happiness."[3]

People respond to kind and caring words. It never fails. You can bank on that principle.

Becoming a Friend to the End

How do you suppose Philemon reacted to Paul's positive and confident words? I think he did what Paul asked and even passed on the principles to Onesimus. I think Philemon let Onesimus know he still believed in him.

And what happened to this former runaway servant? History has preserved another letter written in A.D. 115 from Ignatius of Antioch to the bishop of Ephesus. And the bishop's name? Onesimus.

Our Onesimus would have been in his seventies when the letter was received. Many scholars believe Bishop Onesimus of Ephesus was the same Onesimus who returned to Philemon. If so, his success and fulfillment in life were due, in large part, to the encouragement he found in his relationships with his loyal friends, Paul and Philemon.

How do you think Onesimus felt when he heard Paul rise to his defense and offer to pay his debt? He must have become more committed to Paul than ever before. And how did it affect Philemon to know that Paul really believed in him? It spurred him on toward a deeper and more meaningful level of commitment.

Have you crossed the Rubicon with anyone? Do you have a loyal friend? One who is open to you? One who feels free to ask a favor?

Do you have a friend who rises to your defense and is committed to you no matter what?

We all have a friend who "sticks closer than a brother" (Prov.

18:24). Jesus Christ is committed to you. He is open. He builds bridges and not barriers.

He stands up for you. He crossed His own Rubicon for you and never looked back. He brings out the best in each of us. And He believes in us and helps us to believe in ourselves.

Like no other person in our lives, Jesus is and always will be a friend to the end.

Staying Accountable

*But, meanwhile, also prepare a guest room for me, for
I trust that through your prayers I shall be granted to
you. Epaphras, my fellow prisoner in Christ Jesus,
greets you, as do Mark, Aristarchus, Demas, Luke, my
fellow laborers. The grace of our Lord Jesus Christ be
with your spirit. Amen.*

—*Philemon 22–25*

CHAPTER TWELVE

THE MARK OF A TRUE FRIEND

I AM AN ALL-AMERICAN BOY at heart. Part of the proof is the fact that I drive a General Motors automobile. I always have and suppose I always will. One of the reasons I drive an American car is the super service department at my local dealership. Periodically, I take my car in for a checkup. The service manager makes certain my automobile is properly maintained so that it will continue to run smoothly.

My wife and I own our home. Or I should say, the mortgage holder owns it. Periodically, we give it an inspection. Once we made some repairs on the roof. It wasn't leaking . . . yet! Some wood was rotting around one of the eaves, and it was only a matter of time before bigger problems arose. So, we did some preventive maintenance.

I have a body. Not much of one, some might argue! But a body nevertheless. Every six months to a year I go to my physician for a complete physical in order to make certain everything is fine and to detect any possible problems. Along with getting a physical exam, I watch my diet and try to take good care of myself. I practice preventive medicine.

Much of what goes wrong with my car or my home or my body does so because of neglect. No checkup. No maintenance. If these are necessary for cars, homes, and bodies, they are also needed in our relationships with others.

It is wise from time to time for husbands and wives and even friends to sit down with each other and examine their relationship. Lasting relationships are those that practice preventive maintenance.

The Need for Accountability

I am accountable to my wife. I do not just go my own way, telling her that where I go and what I do are none of her business. They *are* her business. We are one. We have a unique relationship out of all our others because we must answer to each other for what we do, where we go, and how we behave.

We are accountable at the office. We do not just show up at work whenever we feel like it. There are schedules to be followed if we expect to be paid. We also do what is required, not just what is particularly enjoyable for us. Profitable businesses are successful in large part due to the insistence on accountability.

Schools run on accountability. Students must turn in homework, write certain papers, and take scheduled tests. No one graduates or earns a degree without completing the required assignments.

What about the athletic arena? If an athlete refuses to attend practice sessions, he or she doesn't play in the games. In the sport of basketball, a player who commits five fouls in a single game is taken out of the game by the official. Athletes must answer to officials, umpires, and referees on the playing field.

We are held responsible for our finances. There are monthly bills to pay. If we fall behind, certain unpleasant consequences result.

Since accountability is a significant part of everything we do, it's strange that in regard to our friends, we often don't see the need for it. We have the attitude that "what I do is my business." Is it any wonder there is an epidemic of shallow and broken relationships today?

When I was a teenager, my friend Jack Graham and I began to notice what was happening around us. We watched some of our peers disintegrate, destroying their lives with such things as alcohol, drugs, and illicit sex.

Jack and I became accountable to each other. We didn't know what to call it, but we made a promise to God and to each other that we would help each other stay clean. We checked up weekly on each other.

To this day, although we began almost thirty years ago and for many years were separated by fifteen hundred miles, he is still my best friend. And we still hold each other accountable.

The Unexamined Life

Attitudes such as self-righteousness, self-sufficiency, and self-centeredness will destroy a relationship. To counter these tendencies, accountability between close friends is an absolute necessity. The lack of it has caused the downfall of a lot of people with great promise and has kept many potential friendships on a superficial level.

Patrick Morley talks about accountability in his best-selling book *The Man in the Mirror*.

The British steamer, the Titanic, was considered by experts to be unsinkable. One of the largest sea disasters in history occurred when the Titanic struck the hidden part of an iceberg on its maiden voyage during the night of April 14, 1912. Fifteen hundred people perished as the submerged part of a mountain of ice ripped open a three-hundred-foot-long gash in the hull of what was then the greatest ocean liner in the world.

An iceberg is one of nature's most beautiful and dangerous phenomena. What we see of these masses of broken-off glaciers is beautiful—like the "best foot" each of us puts forward with our friends. But only one-eighth to one-tenth of an iceberg is visible—the rest is hidden below the surface of the water. And that is where the danger lurks.

Like an iceberg, the beautiful part of our lives is that tenth or so which people can see. What's below the surface, however, is where we live our real lives—lives often hidden from the scrutiny of other Christians. The jagged subsurface edges of our secret lives often rip open our relationships and damage our spiritual lives. What is unseen and not carefully examined can sink us when we are unaccountable for those areas of our lives.

. . . Most of our conversation revolves around the cliche level of life—news, sports, and weather. But this is the tip of the iceberg—the "visible" you. The "real" you wrestles with gut-wrenching issues in the key areas of our lives every day, and we each need someone to help us navigate around the submerged dangers of an unexamined life.[1]

Is there someone in your life who has earned the right to ask some uncomfortable questions and who knows enough about your life to know just which questions to ask?

In the same way, have you invested enough in the life of another so that you can gently let the person know when something is amiss? Solomon said, "Faithful *are* the wounds of a friend,/ But the kisses of an enemy *are* deceitful" (Prov. 27:6).

What Is Accountability?

Accountability is the ability to be open and allow a small number of trusted, loyal, and committed friends to speak the truth in love to us. All of us need someone from whom we can receive loving counsel and correction and to whom we are close enough to give it.

Close relationship becomes possible when we have made an investment of time and interest in another's life. When we have shown someone the depth of our caring through time, effort, and love, we have earned the right to lovingly challenge or confront when necessary. In the same way, when we know how much someone cares for us, we are able to listen to loving confrontation. Answering to others is uncomfortable for many of us. It is not in our nature to want to be held liable for our attitudes or actions.

Too many never become accountable to anyone else because of a warped idea of what it really involves. Some of us fear it because we misunderstand it, thinking only of put-downs, criticisms, or rebuke from those who take delight in sitting in the judge's seat.

I am not talking about open season on each other. It isn't wise or beneficial to disclose our innermost secrets to anyone and everyone. Some people seem to have the gifts of criticism, gossip, and judging the faults of others.

Accountability hinges instead on mercy and grace. It cannot be effective without the forgiveness that loving friends offer each other.

Friends Should Be Vulnerable

Accountability to each other requires that we be transparent with our true friends. Everyone needs someone with whom to be genuinely open and honest. This vulnerability carries with it the risk of being wounded. But deep relationships cannot be achieved without it.

When I think of true friendships, the story that comes to mind most often is that of David and Jonathan. The relationship they shared is a powerful example of what true, committed relationships are all about.

First Samuel beautifully records the depth of their friendship:

> Now when he [David] had finished speaking to Saul, the soul of Jonathan was knit to the soul of David, and Jonathan loved him as his own soul. . . . Then Jonathan and David made a covenant, because he loved him as his own soul. And Jonathan took off the robe that was on him and gave it to David, with his armor, even to his sword and his bow and his belt (vv. 18:1, 3–4).

I like what author Richard Exley had to say about these words from 1 Samuel:

When Jonathan disrobed, he made himself transparent to David. It was his way of saying that he had nothing to

hide. . . . A friendship built on anything else is just a sham—
a make-believe friendship between two people who are
pretending to be something other than who they really are.
As C. S. Lewis said, "Eros will have naked bodies; friendships
naked personalities."

When Jonathan gave David his weapons—his sword,
his bow, and his belt—he made himself vulnerable. He was
at David's mercy. He had no way to defend himself. So it
is in a true friendship. When we share our deepest self with
our friend, we are giving him weapons with which he can
destroy us. It is the ultimate act of trust, and it is what
distinguishes the truly great friendships from those that are
just average.[2]

Do you have a friend like that? Someone with whom you
can be completely open and vulnerable? Someone whose soul
is knitted to yours? This is the kind of friendships that God
wants for us—friendships that will keep us accountable for our
actions.

Friends Should Be Approachable

Close fellowship also requires that we be available to each
other, that we be approachable.

Many people keep others at bay through sheer busyness.
They are too swamped with activity to slow down long enough
and listen to what they need to hear. This may be deliberate or
subconscious, but the effect is the same. Others are kept at arm's
length, and the friendship and closeness that should be there
simply aren't.

Others put up a defensive wall that is almost tangible. They say, without having to use words, "Keep your distance." And people usually do.

Effective closeness and accountability happen when friends are willing to say, "Nothing is more important than you. I will put this aside for now. What is on your mind?"

If you want to be a true friend to others, learn to be approachable. Let them know that you care, that you will always be there for them. Let them know your commitment to open and honest dialogue within the relationship. And pledge to never turn a deaf ear on a friend in need.

You'll be surprised to see how much deeper your relationships become when you take time to be there for others.

Friends Should Be Truthful

Those who are accountable to each other must also be truthful with others and themselves. Many never allow themselves to enter an accountable relationship because of self-deception. They are always convinced that it is someone else's fault when a relationship becomes bruised or broken.

It is impossible to become accountable to each other unless we are both committed to the truth, however painful it may seem. We never have to be afraid of the truth. It liberates. It sets us free.

Many of us have personal friends who are on a collision course with corruption and disaster. But we let them go. Sometimes we don't care enough to confront them, and other times we are afraid of offending them. But if we are to be a true friend to others, we need to get past our apathy and past our fears. We need to confront when we see them heading for trouble.

To the church in Galatia, Paul wrote, "Brethren, if a man is overtaken in any trespass, you who are spiritual restore such a one in a spirit of gentleness, considering yourself lest you also be tempted" (Gal. 6:1).

Michael is a good example of a man who cared enough to risk losing a valued friendship rather than watch his friend get hurt.

Michael's friend Jim was a troubleshooter for a large organization in Texas. As a Christian, Jim was devoted to his wife and children, and he was an active worker in his church.

Over the course of time, Michael noticed that Jim and his secretary, Amy, were spending a lot of unnecessary time with each other, going on errands together, and talking at length after quitting time.

Michael cared about Jim and his family, and he was concerned about what others might be saying. One afternoon, he gathered his courage, went into Jim's office, and said to him, "You know, Jim, when a frog is dropped into a pot of boiling water, it will immediately jump out. It feels the intensity of the heat and knows better than to stay in the fire. But when it is put into tepid water, and the heat is turned up very gradually, the frog will unknowingly boil to death. The heat sneaks up on it, and it doesn't realize the danger.

"I see the same thing happening to you, and I'm concerned for your safety. You've been spending a lot of time with Amy. I know your intentions are not bad, and I know you love your wife. But I want you to be aware of the danger. If you're honest with yourself, you probably find yourself becoming more and more attracted to her, and she is likely feeling the same about you. The water is slowly getting hotter, and I really don't want either of you to get burned."

Michael had been a bundle of nerves, not knowing what Jim

would say to this. Would he be told to mind his own business? Would he get a blank stare? Actually, the relationship had been such that his friend knew he cared. The answer he received was, "Mike, thanks. Thanks for caring. I've been walking too close to the edge with this. Thank you for caring enough to call me on it."

The "innocent" rendezvous with the secretary stopped, and Jim's relationship with his wife soon became better than ever. Michael had earned the right to confront his friend through years of working, worshiping, and relaxing together. And as a friend, he cared enough to confront.

Friends Should Be Teachable

Relationships that benefit from accountability do so because the parties involved are also teachable. We all have much to learn from each other. It is a dangerous time in any interpersonal relationship when someone feels he or she knows it all and no longer possesses a teachable spirit.

In a letter that Paul wrote to Philemon's home church, he urges, "Let the word of Christ dwell in you richly as you teach and admonish one another with all wisdom" (Col. 3:16 NIV). In Romans 15:14, Paul also writes, "I myself am convinced, my brothers, that you yourselves are full of goodness, complete in knowledge and competent to instruct one another" (NIV).

Being teachable requires a spirit of humility. Paul says of this subject: "Be completely humble and gentle" (Eph. 4:2 NIV), and "in humility consider others better than yourselves" (Phil. 2:3 NIV).

We've all run across people who think they know all they

need to know. They are so sure of themselves and confident in their opinions that nobody even tries to argue with them anymore. They've built a reputation that follows them wherever they go.

But more often than not, they are the people who know the least. And though they exude an air of confidence, they are really quite insecure. Their know-it-all facade is a mask covering the uncertainty that lies beneath it.

True friendship demands that we overcome our fears and insecurities and let others see beneath the surface—beneath the masks we wear. It demands that we honestly admit our short-comings. And it demands that we be willing to learn.

The Joy of Accountability

We now arrive at the final paragraph of this enlightening letter on interpersonal relationships. I can almost see Philemon now, with chin cupped in hand, as he reads, "But, meanwhile, also prepare a guest room for me, for I trust that through your prayers I shall be granted to you" (v. 22).

Paul is a bit subtle here, but the message is loud and clear: "I am going to come by to check up on you. I am coming by to see how you and Onesimus are doing in your relationship." There is a saying that goes, "You must inspect what you expect." Paul intends to do just that.

How do you think this motivated Philemon? How are you motivated when someone you love, admire, and respect will find out something about you? The prospect of Paul's upcoming visit no doubt prompted Philemon to do the right thing in his relationship with the remorseful Onesimus. There is something about knowing that we will one day have to answer for our actions that propels us to be more conscientious about our task.

There is a subtle insight into this letter that is apparent only in the original Greek. Paul requests of Philemon, "But, meanwhile, also prepare a guest room for me, for I trust that through your prayers I shall be granted to you." The "your" and "you" are plural. This is significant. Paul is reminding Philemon that others will be watching.

Accountability is an essential ingredient to true, lasting friendships. Only when we learn to be accountable to others, and to hold others accountable, will we understand what it means to be true brothers and sisters in Christ.

CHAPTER THIRTEEN

A GLORIOUS REUNION

*H*OW DO YOU ACT when you know you will have to answer to others? Does it keep you on your best behavior? Does it make you want to do what's right? It should. That's what accountability is all about.

Support groups know this well. Most weight reduction programs are built around the principle of accountability. Once a week these groups get together to check up on each other and monitor each other's progress. And it works. Just knowing that they will be seeing the group within a few days almost always keeps people on track in their diets.

The same holds true for Alcoholics Anonymous. They hold each other accountable in their meetings. And more often than not, it builds a kind of willpower within people that they wouldn't otherwise have. They stay sober because they don't want to disappoint their friends.

The principle should also hold true for churches. Effective pastors know the importance of accountability within their congregations. They work at helping people connect with each other, encouraging them to meet together outside services, holding each other accountable for their actions. Without it, Christians can easily get off track in their walk with God.

Paul knows how important it is for friends to hold each other accountable, and he ends his letter to Philemon with greetings from five of their mutual friends. This group no doubt works at keeping each other accountable. They lean on each other for support. And Paul is subtly (or not so subtly) reminding Philemon of his connection with the group. He is letting Philemon know that if he chooses to do the wrong thing, he has good friends in the faith to whom he will have to answer.

He writes, "Epaphras, my fellow prisoner in Christ Jesus, greets you, as do Mark, Aristarchus, Demas, Luke, my fellow laborers" (vv. 23–24).

These are names Philemon recognizes. And reading their greetings on paper appeals to his sense of loyalty. He knows he will be seeing them again, and he will do anything to keep from disappointing the group.

Aristarchus: The Affirming One

Paul mentions these five people for another reason as well. He is a genius at human relationships, and each of these men illustrates a truth that Paul has been driving home throughout his correspondence with Philemon. Each man represents a paragraph in the letter.

For example, Paul began by showing the importance of a pat on the back. It is interesting that he now brings up the name of Aristarchus, his traveling companion on the third missionary journey.

Paul and Aristarchus had a connection that only people who have traveled long distances together can know. Their friendship had weathered heat, cold, hunger, and persecutions. Aristarchus evidently didn't flinch. He traveled to Rome with Paul, and he had even been arrested in Ephesus. Such loyalty isn't found every day or with just anyone. To Paul, the name Aristarchus meant "affirmation."

Luke: The Winning One

Paul also brings up the name of Luke. Dr. Luke, we might call him. In his letter to the Colossians, Paul calls Luke "the beloved physician" (Col. 4:14).

Is your doctor one you wouldn't give up for anything? One who knows you and genuinely cares about you? One who makes house calls? Well, now we're out of the realm of reality, but Paul had a doctor who went beyond house calls. He had Luke.

Luke was a Gentile. In that day, most Jews would have had no dealings with him. But Paul wasn't your average Jew. He saw people through Christ's eyes, not those of society.

Luke accompanied Paul on his second missionary journey and tended to his physical needs, which must have kept him busy. More than once, Paul was stoned and left for dead. He had a physical disorder many believe was either epilepsy or failing eyesight. Luke was always there by his side, and there is no doubt that his health skills added years to Paul's life.

Philemon knew this, and reading Luke's name may have called to mind Paul's words a few paragraphs earlier: "He is now profitable to you and to me." Luke's name is a vivid reminder of the win-win philosophy of relationships depicted earlier in the letter.

Mark: The Forgiven One

Paul has also stressed the importance of forgiveness in our

relationships, and he now mentions a man named Mark. Young Mark was with him on the first journey departing from Antioch. But Mark quit. He went AWOL when the going got tough. And his failure wasn't easy to accept for a get-it-done, type A kind of guy like Paul.

Twelve years have now passed, and this is the first mention of Mark in any of Paul's writings. Obviously, they have buried the hatchet, and he is back in Paul's good graces. We see this in Paul's later letter to Timothy when he says, "Only Luke is with me. Get Mark and bring him with you, for he is useful to me for ministry" (2 Tim. 4:11).

Mark knew what it meant to be accountable, and he knew what it meant to be forgiven. Paul's forgiveness helped Mark to forgive himself. As one speaker asked, "How can you make a man without forgiveness?" Mark went on to "make something of himself," and he was even the author of the gospel that carries his name.

The mention of Mark's name spoke volumes to Philemon's heart as he continued to read this letter. If he followed Paul's example, how could he do anything less than to take Onesimus back?

Epaphras: The Committed One

Paul has also underscored the need for commitment in our relationships. So it comes as no surprise that he mentions Epaphras. His life was characterized by an uncommon dedication to his friends.

In his letter to the Colossians, Paul says, "Epaphras, who is one of you, a bondservant of Christ, greets you, always laboring fervently for you in prayers, that you may stand perfect and complete in all the will of God. For I bear him witness that he has a great zeal for you, and those who are in Laodicea, and those in Hierapolis" (4:12–13).

Who in your life sweats in prayer for you, wanting desperately for you to be a friend and fellow worker with God? Epaphras was this kind of friend to Paul and to others. He even went to Rome and voluntarily shared Paul's imprisonment there. He was also a friend of Philemon's. Philemon may have known what Paul was getting at the moment he read Epaphras's name.

Demas: The Fallen One

The inclusion of Demas's name adds a bit of irony to the letter. And its message speaks more to us than it did to Philemon. Although even Paul couldn't have known it at the time, Demas is a haunting example of what can happen without accountability in our lives.

Paul will write years later in his second letter to Timothy, "For Demas has forsaken me, having loved this present world, and has departed for Thessalonica" (2 Tim. 4:10). Demas is a sad commentary on the fact that our spiritual health and direction can suffer without accountability.

By mentioning these five friends, each representative of a requirement for successful relationships, Paul is reminding us of the need we have for each other and the difference that mutual affirmation can make in our lives.

We All Need Grace

Paul concludes his letter to Philemon with a benediction: "The grace of the Lord Jesus Christ be with your spirit" (v. 25). What is he saying? We need grace. We require it to live with others and to live with ourselves. Grace lets us break free from the shackles of our mistakes. It frees us to live the joyful, effective lives we are meant to live.

Grace can be defined as unmerited favor. It is getting what we do not deserve. Not one of us can do enough or become good enough to earn a relationship with the Creator and a permanent life with Him. But His grace gives it to us freely.

John MacArthur tells the story of a man who had spent his entire life dreaming of someday going on a cruise. As a youngster, he salivated at advertisements for luxury cruises across the ocean. But because he was from a poor family, it seemed to be a dream far out of reach.

Then one day he started saving money, counting every penny, in hopes to someday realize the dream. There were times when he wondered if he would ever have enough, and so he often sacrificed small comforts in order to stretch his resources a little farther.

Finally, after years of saving, he had enough to purchase a ticket. He went to a travel agent and picked out a cruise that was especially attractive. He could hardly contain his excitement as he paid for the ticket and started packing for the trip.

The problem was, he was still a poor man. Almost everything he had went toward the purchase of the ticket. He knew he would have no money to pay for meals during the trip. So he took what little he had left and bought a week's worth of peanut butter and bread for the trip.

The first few days of the cruise were thrilling. He ate peanut butter sandwiches alone in his room each morning and spent the rest of his time relaxing in the sunlight and fresh air, just delighted to be aboard the ship.

But by the middle of the week, peanut butter sandwiches began to taste like cardboard. All around him, people were dining on luxurious meals, and he could hardly stand watching them another day. So he approached a porter.

"Tell me how I might get one of those meals! I'm dying for some decent food, and I'll do anything you say to earn it!" he told the porter.

"Why, sir," the porter answered, "don't you have a ticket for this cruise?"

"Certainly," said the man. "But I spent everything I had for that ticket. I have nothing left with which to buy food."

"But, sir," said the porter, "didn't you realize? Meals are included with your passage. You may eat as much as you like!"

After telling the story, John MacArthur adds,

Lots of Christians live like that man. Not realizing the unlimited provisions that are theirs in Christ, they munch on stale scraps. There's no need to live like that! Everything we could ever want or need is included in the cost of admission—and the Savior has already paid it for us.[1]

God's grace is the greatest gift we could ever imagine getting. If He has forgiven us of so much, we must be willing to offer that same kind of grace and love to those who fail us.

Paul is making it plain to Philemon that if he is going to forgive Onesimus, he is going to need an extra portion of grace to accomplish it. He needs the grace to go forward and the wisdom to see that he cannot do it in his own strength. It is really not in our human natures to forgive and to forget, but the power of God in our lives is greater than our human natures.

The Spirit of Forgiveness

Paul asked that the grace of God be with Philemon's "spirit." My spirit is the real me. It is the part of me that makes me different from all the other created order, the part that can connect with God. This relationship gives us the grace we need to successfully live with others. With this reminder, Paul closes the letter to his friend and brother Philemon.

And what happened? Did Philemon do what Paul asked? Did he receive Onesimus with open arms as a "beloved brother"? Did he forgive? Did he forget? The answers to these questions are shrouded in silence. Quite honestly, we do not know.

But really, it's not important that we know. The question for us is not, "What did Philemon do?"; rather, it is, "What will you do with the Onesimus in your own life?"

Everyone knows someone who needs forgiveness. We all disappoint each other from time to time in one way or another, but if we make a mistake in our relationships, why should we not try to err on the side of grace and mercy rather than on the side of judgment? Ultimately, we know that we need to decide to do the right thing. We need to look past the transgression, take the person by the hand, and forgive for his or her sake and for ours.

Paving the Way for Relationship

We began this book by looking at three basic elements of successful relationships in life: we need to be connected with the Source, which is God; the switch, which represents ourselves; and the socket, which is others. And now we come full circle and look at this truth again.

We are repeatedly told in the Scriptures to love *God* with all our heart, soul, mind, and strength, and to love our *neighbors* as *ourselves.* Jesus even said that these are the first and second greatest commandments (Matt. 22:36–40).

Our first and most important relationship is with God. He is the source of our power, the glue that holds all of our relationships together. Without Him, we will never gain true love and intimacy with others.

Second, we need to be at peace with ourselves, to be in right relationship internally. Accepting ourselves is a prerequisite to effectively reaching out to those around us.

Third, we must be connected to others. We must be willing to forgive and forget, to look out for each other's interests, to be willing to commit on a deep level, and to hold each other accountable for the things we do. We need to have friendships that go far beneath the surface and reach into our very souls.

The greatest lessons of life are in the small, seemingly insignificant, and often inconvenient interruptions. Looking back, I'm thankful the desk lamp did not come on in my hotel room in Oakland at three o'clock that particular morning. If it had, I would have missed a magnificent lesson that has enabled me to relate better to my wife and children as well as those with whom I work and play.

We are made to shine. But until we are plugged in to the Source, we do not really live; we simply exist.

God, our very Source, is the initiator of all our relationships. To identify with us, He laid aside His glory, humbled Himself, and came to where we are. He clothed Himself in skin and lived with us for thirty-three years in the person of Jesus. He walked with us, talked with us, ate with us, and yet He was not contaminated by our sin.

He reached out to the rejects and defended the dejected. He

loved the lonely, and He still does. He forgives the sinner. He gives the failure a second chance and then another and still another. He gives us the chance to escape our past. And He taught us how to extend that same love and forgiveness to others.

He was willing to give up everything He had known—His glory, His security, and His surroundings. And the result? He will change the lives and destinies of all who take him as their Lord and Savior.

The Ultimate Relationship

So now we come to a final hard question. What are you going to do with Jesus? How are you going to deal with what you know about Him? Will you let Him pave the way to your appointment with God, as Paul paved the way for Onesimus to return to Philemon?

Jesus is our only hope of salvation. He came to earth and died on a Roman cross for our sins, paving the way for a beautiful reunion between the Creator and the creation. He was buried in the ground and came bursting out of the grave three days later. His life is no fairy tale; it is recorded history. And He says that the way to God is through Him. There is no other way (see John 14:6).

So what will you do with Him? How are you going to answer His call for reconciliation?

Calvary stands on the time line of history as the most significant event ever to take place. In a matter of seconds, everything changed.

Author Max Lucado paints a beautiful portrait of that moment in time:

You can't go to the cross with just your head and not your heart. It doesn't work that way. Calvary is not a mental trip. It's not an intellectual exercise. It's not a divine calculation or a cold theological principle.

It's a heart-splitting hour of emotion.

Don't walk away from it dry-eyed and unstirred. Don't just straighten your tie and clear your throat. Don't allow yourself to descend Calvary cool and collected.

Please . . . pause. Look again.

Those are nails in those hands. That's *God* on that cross. It's us who put him there.

Peter knew it. John knew it. Mary knew it.

They knew a great price was being paid. They knew who really pierced his side. They also somehow knew that history was being remade.

That's why they wept. They *saw* the Savior.[2]

Have you *seen* the Savior? Have you been to Calvary and taken the hand of forgiveness extended your way?

Jesus offers us a brand new life, a chance to start over again. He offers us a glorious hand of reconciliation. Saying yes to Him is the best decision we will ever make.

SECTION I: THE ART OF CONNECTING

Chapter One: The Source

1. List some ways that we can be messengers of grace and peace to others. Read Colossians 3:15; 1 Peter 4:10; Mark 9:50; and 2 Corinthians 13:11.

2. What are some ways in which we try to find meaning in our lives apart from God?

3. A teenager was spotted in a mall wearing a T-shirt that said, "Soccer is my life." What would your friends say is your life? See Deuteronomy 30:19–20.

4. What does the story of the prodigal son say about God's knowledge of us and what He wants us to know about Himself?

5. To what extent do you see God as a caring Father? Is there anything blocking your acceptance of His love for you? See Psalm 31:7; Psalm 66:20; and Isaiah 1:18.

6. What kinds of things today beckon us to take our inheritance from God—eternal life—and squander it?

7. The "covering" of a credit card gives us the freedom to have things that will be paid for at a separate time. What freedom has Christ's blood given us for our lives on earth that we otherwise wouldn't have? Read Galatians 5:13 and 1 Peter 2:16.

8. Isaiah 33:6 tells us that God "will be the sure foundation for your times,/ a rich store of salvation and wisdom and knowledge" (NIV).
   a) What is the key to this treasure? See Isaiah 33:6b.

   b) How do we have or get the fear of the Lord? Read Psalm 86:11 and Isaiah 11:2-3.

   c) How does 1 Samuel 12:24 encourage us to have an undivided heart?

9. Read Isaiah 12:2–3. Is there an area where you can turn a fear over to God in trust? Look for the joy He gives you this week as you "draw water from the wells of salvation" (NIV). Jesus told a Samaritan woman of His willingness to give her "living water" (John 4:10). Her life had been messed up by six men. What aspect of your life can be healed by the Source of eternal life?

10. Acts 17:28 declares, "In Him we live and move and have our being." For what are you especially thankful today?

Chapter Two: The Switch

1. Read Romans 12:3 (NIV). What things prevent us from thinking of ourselves with "sober judgment"?

2. If the prophet Samuel told you, "You will be changed into a different person," what would be different about you? What would you like to have changed? Read 1 Samuel 10:6. What caused Saul to be changed into a different person?

3. Is there any relationship that you'd like to change? How can you practice the "being comes before doing" idea here?

4. Is something in your life imprisoning you? How can becoming a "prisoner of Jesus Christ" change this?

5. Look up Psalm 71:5; Proverbs 3:26; and Jeremiah 17:7. What is the source of confidence?

6. What does it mean to die to oneself? What would it mean for you specifically?

7. Satan hates us and is constantly accusing us. If we listen to him long enough, we won't like ourselves very much. What might he be telling you, and what is God saying instead? Read 1 John 3:1 and Romans 8:1, 16.

8.   What would it do for your self-esteem for several heads of
      state to call you a friend? How much more should it mean
      to us that the Creator of the universe calls us His friend and
      tells us His business (see John 15:15)? How can we come to
      the place where this makes more of an impact on our lives?

9.   You need to take seriously the words of Zephaniah 3:17: "He
      will take great delight in you/. . . he will rejoice over you with
      singing" (NIV). What would God sing about you?

10.   Psalm 139:17–18 states that God's thoughts to (or concern-
      ing) me outnumber the grains of sand. How should this
      statement affect my view of myself?

Chapter Three: The Socket

1. When God took the concept of family and incorporated it into the early church, what changes were made in the Christians' lives? See Acts 2:42–47.

2. What is one thing you could do this week to foster more of a spirit of community among your family at home or at church?

3. Read Ephesians 4:15–16 (NIV). What do you want to be when you "grow up into him"?

4. John 13:35 states, "All men will know that you are my disciples, if you love one another" (NIV). This is what marks us as belonging to Him. Are there any counterfeit ways we try to identify ourselves with Him?

5. In Philippians 2:2 (NIV), Paul asks the Philippians to be like-minded, have the same love, and be one in spirit and purpose. Why and how can they do this?

6. Some of the things that hinder fellow workers are not having a common goal, not obeying the boss, and judging instead of working. What can counteract these tendencies? See Philippians 3:13; James 4:12; John 14:23; and Romans 14:4.

7. Read Hebrews 10:24–25 (NIV). How can we "spur one another on"?

8. Read 2 Timothy 2:3–4 (NIV). If you are a good soldier of Christ Jesus, what would it mean for you to be "involved in civilian affairs"?

9. What are some of the hardships you've endured as a soldier of Christ? In what ways can you identify with the experiences described in 2 Corinthians 6:3–10?

Section II: A Pat on the Back

Chapter Four: Learn to Affirm

1.   Think of a time when you received a pat on the back. Who gave it to you, and how did it affect your relationship with the person?

2.   How is it possible to be blinded to reality or stunted in our personal growth by accepting affirmation from others indiscriminately? Read Judges 4:17–21 for an extreme example.

3.   James 5:16 tells us that "the prayer of a righteous man is powerful and effective" (NIV). What keeps us from praying more often and more fervently for others?

4.   Paul had undoubtedly read 1 Samuel 12:23 many times, and he obviously had taken it to heart. Why is this particular sin described as being "against the Lord"?

5.   a) Read 2 Chronicles 30:27. What did it take for their prayers to reach heaven?

b) Study 2 Chronicles 30:13–14, 18–20, 22. How do our prayers reach heaven?

6. Read Psalm 35:18. What does open, public thanksgiving to God do for us and for others?

7. Why is it so easy to show favoritism without thinking about it? What can we do to counteract this human tendency?

8. *Philemon* means "the loving one." How had he lived up to his name in the past? How powerful is a name in influencing a person's character and actions?

Chapter Five: Refreshment for the Heart

1. a) What stumbling blocks does Satan try to throw in front of your efforts to share Christ with others?

    b) What can you do to overcome them? Study Ephesians 6:10–18 and 2 Timothy 1:6–7.

2. What "good things" are in us because of Christ? Look at Colossians 3:15–16, and Ephesians 3:20.

3. Does the idea of a full understanding of what we have in Christ seem out of your grasp? Ask God to reveal more of Himself, His love, and His will to you today. See Ephesians 1:7–9.

4. Is there anyone whose love is giving you joy and encouragement? What would it do for the person to hear about it from you? See 2 Corinthians 7:13.

5. Who in your circle of family or friends would say that you have refreshed their hearts? What have you said or done that would cause them to say this?

6. What is it about your life that Christ has refreshed?

7.   Read 1 Corinthians 16:18. How can you give recognition to those who are encouragers?

8.   Step out on a limb, and give a stranger with whom you have contact a genuine compliment. Note what happens.

SECTION III: WIN-WIN RELATIONSHIPS

Chapter Six: The Games People Play

1. Study Proverbs 22:24–25. Why is being "furious" a snare to a person's soul?

2. Describe a time in your life when you've seen Proverbs 15:1 in action.

3. John 4:1–42 tells the story of the woman at the well. Read John 4:10. What is Jesus asking for in your life? What does He want you to ask of Him?

4. The account of King Jehoshaphat's battle against a vastly superior army is told in 2 Chronicles 20. List at least four things that he did in the face of discouragement.

5. Colossians 3:18–24 gives practical advice for successful relationships.
    a) If you were consciously working for the Lord, not for men, would you do anything differently?

    b) Which one of these commands poses the most difficulty for you?

6. Proverbs 10:12 asserts, "Hatred stirs up strife,/ But love covers all sins." What could you cover with love today?

7. Nehemiah 4 tells a story of cooperation during the rebuilding of the Jerusalem wall. Those who were working together were defending their very lives. How does their situation compare with ours in today's world?

8. Why is cooperation sometimes difficult when we have so much to gain from it?

Chapter Seven: The Only Way to Win

1. Think about the last time you tried to win someone to your point of view. How did you go about it?

2. Philemon had to look at Onesimus with new eyes. How easy or hard is it to allow a person to break out of an old mold and become someone different? In what ways can we accomplish this?

3. What would you need to do to take Christ's yoke on yourself? He says that it's easy. Do you believe Him? What is it that He wants you personally to learn? Read Matthew 11:28–29.

4. James 3:17 says that we should be "willing to yield." How easy is it to confuse yielding our convictions with yielding our preferences?

5. Is there anyone who is depending on you for support and encouragement? What are you doing for that person in this area?

6. Read 2 Timothy 2:21. In what ways are you "useful for the Master"? Is there an area in which you are "useless"? If so, what can you do about it?

7. Philemon had to stop using Onesimus and treat him like a person instead. Might there be someone in your life who needs to be loved, not used?

8. Read James 1:27. How can you be sure that your religion is "pure and undefiled"? What kinds of things mix into religion to defile it?

9. Study Philippians 2:5–11. Is there anyone in your life with whom you are "grasping" to be equal? What would it mean in your life to have the nature of a servant?

10. Read Colossians 3:2–3. Do you know anyone whose "life is hidden with Christ in God"? What is the most outstanding quality of this person?

SECTION IV: BURYING THE HATCHET

Chapter Eight: Looking for a Fresh Start

1.   What is your latest memory of burying the hatchet with someone? What had to be done? Who initiated it?

2.   Study Psalm 51:16–17 What "sacrifices" might we be inclined to offer the Lord other than a "contrite heart" and a "broken spirit"?

3.   Is there someone you believe has "reached the limit" in expecting you to forgive? What can you do to break this barrier?

4.   Matthew 18:23–35 tells the story of a servant who was forgiven much, then refused to forgive someone else. Why do we have a tendency not to want to forgive when we've been forgiven of so much?

5.   How do you know if you've forgiven someone from your heart? (See Matt. 18:35.)

6.   Study the story of Abigail and David in 1 Samuel 25. What are some of the things she did to make things right again?

7. Is there someone you need to ask for forgiveness? What is making it difficult? How can you overcome this?

8. Read Mark 15:37–38. Do you think the priests immediately understood the significance of the torn curtain? What does it mean to you to be welcomed into the Holy of Holies, into God's presence?

9. Read Luke 17:3–5. How does this statement from Jesus give you encouragement as to God's acceptance of you?

Chapter Nine: The Hand of Forgiveness

1. Paul never actually used the word *forgive* in talking to Philemon. What actions was Philemon asked to demonstrate, though, that would show forgiveness?

2. a) Study 2 Corinthians 2:6–11. What can happen to a person when others refuse to forgive him or her?

   b) Satan is all about accusing and condemning. How does refusing to forgive play into his hands? See 2 Corinthians 2:11.

3. Do the truths in 1 John 1:9 enable you to live a more joyful, effective life for God? What does this verse tell you about His attitude toward you?

4. From Micah 7:18 we learn that God doesn't stay angry forever, and that He delights to show mercy. Ask Him to give you the same personality traits.

5. Read Hebrews 12:14,15.
   a) What things can you do today in order to "pursue peace" with everyone?

   b) Is there a particular "root of bitterness" in a relationship that needs to be uprooted?

6.   How can forgiveness change your family relationships?

7.   Jeremiah 31:34 tells us that God forgives and forgets. How does knowing this affect the way we approach Him?

8.   a)   After Peter's denial of Christ, how did he come to where he was able to forgive himself? See John 21:15–19.

        b)   Is there anything for which you need to forgive yourself?

SECTION V: CROSSING THE RUBICON

Chapter Ten: Building Bridges of Commitment

1. Imagine that Jesus is coming to your house for a five-day visit.

   a) What would you do to prepare? How would you welcome Him, and how would you treat Him?

   b) Now imagine that a person who has treated you badly is coming to see you. How is the reception for that person going to resemble, or differ from, the one you gave Jesus?

2. To what or whom do you have trouble committing? Why is it hard?

3. Study 1 John 3:16. What would it mean today for you to lay down your life for a friend or family member?

4. Jesus won't reject anyone who comes to Him. See John 6:37. How does this knowledge help you approach others with confidence?

5. Do you ever try to hide a part of yourself—your personality, feelings, or past—without stopping first to think why?

What is the worst that could happen if you were open about it? How might a relationship be helped by it?

6. Read John 11:34–36. Are there emotions that you try to hide? How does this affect a relationship?

7. Have you ever paid a debt for someone else? What was the person's response?

8. Has anyone ever given you a large monetary gift, perhaps an inheritance, a mortgage down payment, or the repayment of a loan that you took out? What are your feelings toward the person?

9. Who in your circle of friends or acquaintances has the worst reputation or has at least embarrassed himself or herself? Is there anything you could do to help the person repair the damage and make a clean start?

Chapter Eleven: A Friend to the End

1. Describe a time in your life when someone came to your defense. How did it make you feel?

2. Study Acts 9:26–30. How did Barnabas's standing up for Saul affect both him and the church?

3. Do you know a group of people whose resources are readily available to one another? Who will give whatever is needed? How common or rare is this in your experience?

4. Read Matthew 10:8. Other than salvation, what do you feel is the most significant thing that you have received from Christ lately? Could He be calling you to pass this on to someone else?

5. Read John 21:15–19. Even after Peter had failed miserably, Jesus believed the best about him and assigned him a challenging task. What did this vote of confidence do for Peter?

6. Is there anything that you're being called on to do that seems almost impossible? What resources will you use to accomplish it? See Philippians 4:13.

7. Think of a person in your life who will not perform as you want. For one week, treat the person as if he or she is already coming through. Note any results.

8. It is believed that Philemon's forgiveness of Onesimus changed his life to the extent that he was later in a position of great influence in the Ephesian church. How could Christ's forgiveness change your life? How has it changed things for you?

SECTION VI: STAYING ACCOUNTABLE

Chapter Twelve: The Mark of a True Friend

1. Is there any aspect of your life that needs maintenance right now? What can you do to prevent the necessity of a complete overhaul?

2. a) What is the biggest barrier to accountability with someone else in your life? Is it fear, pride, lack of closeness, or something else?

   b) Ask God to send you someone who will help with an area of your life where you are in danger.

3. Can you remember a time when a close friend "faithfully wounded" you? What was your reaction? How did it affect the friendship? See Proverbs 27:6.

4. In the closest of friendships, self-disclosure is mutual. Is there a lopsided friendship in your life that could benefit from equality in sharing? Which one of you needs to share more?

5. What is the biggest obstacle for you in making time for others? How might you plan to overcome it?

6. Love covers a multitude of sins. See 1 Peter 4:8. How would genuine love take away the fear of being accountable?

7. Read Hebrews 4:13. How would you live differently if you remembered this verse several times a day?

8. Is there anyone who could benefit from your increased concern and involvement in his or her life? What would it take to get to the place where you could help with a serious struggle?

Chapter Thirteen: A Glorious Reunion

1. Do you have a small group of people to whom you are
    accountable? If not, ask God to put you in touch with the
    right people at the right time.

2. Judas was in the most dynamic and world-changing small
    group ever. And yet, he evidently didn't make himself
    accountable to any of the others (see John 12:4–6). Is there
    a precipice that you're heading toward, of which no one else
    is aware?

3. Has your forgiveness made a difference in anyone else's life?

4. a) Does anyone in your circle of friends remind you of
    Epaphras? Who prays for you more than anyone else?

    b) Epaphras shared prison with Paul. What is our attitude
    toward prisoners supposed to be? See Hebrews 13:3.

5. Study Romans 6:14. How does the grace of God free us
    from the shackles of sin?

6. Romans 6:21–22 tells us that the benefit we get from being
    God's slaves leads to holiness, and the result is eternal life.
    What does it mean to be God's slaves? How should this
    affect the way we treat one another?

7.   Read Romans 6:16–23. To whom are you presenting your-
     self for obedience? How do you know that this is the case
     in your life?

8.   Are you giving others the grace and freedom that God gives
     you? Is there anyone you are trying to control, even for the
     person's own good? Why won't this work?

9.   Peter's pride made it hard for him to accept the idea of Jesus'
     doing a menial service for him (see John 13:1–9). Is there
     any attitude of your heart or circumstance in your life that
     is making it hard for you to accept God's gift of mercy and
     grace? How can you deal with it?

Chapter One: The Source
1. Charles Swindoll, *The Grace Awakening* (Dallas: Word, 1990), 9.
2. Swindoll, *The Grace Awakening*, 11–12.

Chapter Three: The Socket
1. Alan Loy McGinnis, *The Friendship Factor* (Minneapolis: Augsburg Publishing House, 1979), 9.
2. McGinnis, *The Friendship Factor*, 9.
3. Douglas L. Fagerstrom and James W. Carlson, *The Lonely Pew* (Grand Rapids: Baker, 1993), 58.
4. Landon Saunders, *How to Win 7 Out of 8 Days a Week* (New York: Dynamis Corp., 1985), 122.
5. Max Lucado, *When God Whispers Your Name* (Dallas: Word, 1994), 177–179.

Chapter Five: Refreshment for the Heart
1. McGinnis, *The Friendship Factor*, 40–41.
2. McGinnis, *The Friendship Factor*, 96.

Chapter Six: The Games People Play
1. Jack Canfield and Mark Victor Hansen, *Chicken Soup for the Soul* (Deerfield Beach, Fla.: Health Communications, 1993), 19–21.
2. Art Williams, *Pushing Up People* (Doraville, Ga.: Parklake Publishers, 1984), 18–19.
3. David A. Seamands, *Healing for Damaged Emotions* (Wheaton, Ill.: Victory Books, 1981), 95.
4. Don A. Aslett, *Clutter's Last Stand* (Cincinnati: Writer's Digest Books, 1984), 257.
5. A. L. Williams, *All You Can Do Is All You Can Do* (Nashville: Thomas Nelson Publishers, 1988), 171.

Chapter Seven: The Only Way to Win
1. Canfield and Hansen, *Chicken Soup for the Soul*, 56–58.
2. Charles R. Swindoll, *Improving Your Serve* (Waco, Tex.: Word, 1981), 119–120.

Chapter Nine: The Hand of Forgiveness
1. Max Lucado, *No Wonder They Call Him the Savior* (Portland: Mult-
   nomah, 1986), 25.
2. Corrie ten Boom, *The Hiding Place* (Uhrichsville, Oh: Barbour and
   Co., 1971), 215.

Chapter Ten: Building Bridges of Commitment
1. McGinnis, *The Friendship Factor*, 185–86.

Chapter Eleven: A Friend to the End
1. Saunders, *How to Win 7 Out of 8 Days a Week*, 22.
2. Bill Hybels, *Who You Are (When No One's Looking)* (Downers Grove,
   Ill.: InterVarsity Press), 85–86.
3. Canfield and Hansen, *Chicken Soup for the Soul*, 32–33.

Chapter Twelve: The Mark of a True Friend
1. Patrick M. Morley, *The Man in the Mirror* (Brentwood, Tenn.:
   Wolgemuth & Hyatt, 1989), 276.
2. Richard Exley, *The Making of a Man* (Tulsa: Honor Books, 1993),
   88.

Chapter Thirteen: A Glorious Reunion
1. John MacArthur, Jr., *Our Sufficiency in Christ* (Dallas: Word, 1991),
   241–42.
2. Lucado, *No Wonder They Call Him the Savior*, 108.

227.8   00003842
Haw   Hawkins
       Tearing Down Walls and Building
       Bridges

227.8   00003842
Haw   Hawkins
       Tearing Down Walls and Building
       Bridges

GAYLORD F